IRONS IN THE FIRE

Also by Russell Brand

My Booky Wook

Russell Brand

IRONS IN THE FIRE

First published in Great Britain in 2007 by Hodder & Stoughton
An Hachette Livre UK company

1

A CIP catalogue record for this title is available from the British Library.

ISBN 978 0340 961360

Typeset in Plantin by Palimpsest Book Production Ltd, Grangemouth, Stirlingshire

Printed and bound by Mackays of Chatham Ltd, Chatham, Kent

Hodder & Stoughton policy is to use papers that are natural, renewable and recyclable products and made from wood grown in sustainable forests. The logging and manufacturing processes are expected to conform to the environmental regulations of the country of origin.

Hodder & Stoughton Ltd
338 Euston Road
London NW1 3BH

www.hodder.co.uk

Dedicated to:

Johnny Lyall's claret and blue army

Introduction

I'm very happy with the publication of this compilation of my *Guardian* columns. Seeing them all together makes me feel like a proper writer with a legacy such as Mark Twain or that fella who wrote the bible; one day perhaps scholars will look back on this volume when trying to understand English football culture early in the third millennium. Although they'd have to be particularly niche academics because I seldom stray from the topics of West Ham United and the antics of the national team, and I'm certain that in both of those areas there are people better qualified than me to provide a balanced account of events. My account is always unbalanced and frightfully biased so unless these as yet unborn, nameless academics crave the solipsistic scribblings of a highly capricious and volatile witness to events at Upton Park and Soho Square they should probably, on uncovering my writings in some excavated knocking shop, keep digging till they reach the works of Richard Lacey or Oliver Holte.

It was an amazing season to chronicle however, from the perspective of an English West Ham fan. East London saw the sacking of Alan Pardew, the take-over by Eggert Magnusson, the arrival of Tevez and Mascherano and the subsequent legal tumult, and a truly epic relegation struggle.

The national team had a new boss in the wake of Sven, the exile and triumphant return of Beckham and for the first time I have been able to join the Press in baiting a manager of England. I can see why they do it because it's a right laugh.

As a personal journey for me as a fan it's been incredible. There was a brief ill-fated period early on where I tried to use the column as a launch pad for a new terrace chant. Retrospectively the notion of West Ham's granite fraternity singing an adaptation of Billy Joel's 'Uptown Girl' was always risible. Occasionally, even now, a sarcastic chant will be slung in my direction as I scuttle to my seat – 'Upton Park' I'll hear; 'We're the Hammers, we're from Upton Park. We're just a bunch of East End Boys, now we're gonna make some effin noise, some effin noise'. Then it'd go into the 'whoah oh oh oh…' bit. There's part of me that still thinks it could've worked. I suppose it's just too damn gay.

Incongruous though it may seem, I have been a football fan all my life but the *Guardian* column coincided with me becoming recognisable from TV, which changed my experience of live matches enormously – almost entirely for the better. Yes, naturally I'm sometimes teased or forced to go through terrifying initiation rituals, like when the occupants of the Centenary Stand made me 'Give 'em a song' and I had to confidently bellow a verse of 'Over land and sea' in a put-on voice three octaves lower than my natural warbling tenor, whilst the raucous chorus jostled, cheered and spilled merry beer. But this was also the season where I received a phone call from Tony Cottee asking me to participate in a charity game against the West Ham team of '86 – including my main footballing heroes Frank McAvennie and Cottee himself. This seemingly splendid offer was in fact something of a poisoned chalice, for were I ever to take to the pitch at the Boleyn it would only be to exhibit myself as a soccer-ninny in front of a group of men I've idolised all my life. Blessedly I was making a film in Hawaii and was unable to attend, although I fear it may be only a temporary reprieve as TC mentioned that these games occur regularly so I may yet be obliged to simultaneously realise a beautiful dream and a humiliating nightmare.

Amazingly for someone who first experienced live football in the early '80s as a tiny boy at my father's side, then as a twitchy adolescent behind the goal with my school friends, then as a solitary junky in the Chicken Run, this was the season where I got to drink in the players' lounge and watch games from executive boxes. I met charming characters who've worked at the club for decades: dear Lesley who runs the bar and once snuck me into the Home dressing room; Jeremy, the announcer who enthusiastically reports home goals and sourly mutters away ones; Tom and Danny in security who've whisked me through the baffling network of secret doors and passages that riddle the stadium – of which you'd never be aware as a fan; and Miranda who's in charge of press and PR and I fancy.

The delirious summit of this new-found access has been meeting players who appear as giants on the field, forever in my mind my father's contemporaries, grown men, but in reality just young lads the age of runners in the TV companies I work with whom I regard as pleasing scamps and ruffle their locks and flip sixpences as treats for worthy endeavours. Christian Dailly is probably a year older than me so it's reasonable that he appears avuncular, but Anton Ferdinand is so young and it's bizarre to chat to this sweet, unassuming chap whilst I'm wearing a replica shirt, feeling like I'm dressed up as him, all alive with adrenalin like when I chat to a good-looking woman.

The absolute zenith occurred when I was on the pitch posing for the cover of this book. Dean Ashton, West Ham's beloved, recently returned centre forward was warming down after a game with one of his preposterous jazz dance routines. I thought, 'Dare I ask? Me? Humble me? Beloved Deano?' I simply had to. I tentatively murmured like an oik, 'Dean, can I have my photo done with you please?' He charmingly agreed and stood beside me whilst I grinned and simpered then to my astonishment when the photographer finished asked me if I could get him a copy, all bashful he was. He even asked me to sign it.

Over the course of the season, which the *Guardian* column has unreliably recorded, I have gone from squinting at claret and blue heroes and praising them in song from the terraces to signing photographs for them. What a journey – why, Homer himself would regard it as improbable and Lunn Poly as uninsurable and yet it happened and here it is. I hope you enjoy reading it as much as I enjoyed writing it. At least as much because it was a total pain in the arse, every column completed with my face pressed against the deadline after frantic exchanges with *Guardian* editors. I hope you enjoy it more than that.

Blowing bubbles in the face of a storm

13 May 2006

Irvine Welsh, a Hibs fan, reckons that supporters of all other clubs would, secretly, prefer to support Hibs, and that their allegiances are a hollow sham that mask Hibs envy. I don't think he's suggesting that his team have supremacy in football terms – that would be mental – rather that they have an intangible, unnameable quality that marks Hibernian out as special. He admits that this delusion is shared by all football fans regarding their own clubs, yet as a West Ham supporter on the day of our first final for 26 years, the notion that there's something magical about West Ham is somehow easy to indulge.

There's something innately romantic about the Hammers; the club's anthem 'Bubbles' has no equal. Most football chants are belligerent, tuneless cries of violent loyalty, or jaunty, playful digs. 'Bubbles' is a wistful and mystical ode to transience and loss – 'they fly so high, nearly reach the sky, then like my dreams they fade and die'. That ain't a clarion call to arms – it makes me want to cry. A song that compares the inevitability of a bubble bursting to lost opportunity and wasted hopes sung by the ICF is a surreal anomaly that makes the paintings of René Magritte look like that picture of the tennis girl scratching her bum.

The only song with similar portent would have to be that of our opponents today, Liverpool, but 'You'll Never Walk Alone' is pedestrian, not only in that it is literally about walking but also its themes are solidarity in adversity, not being afraid of bad weather and other ideas one would expect to encounter being yawped in unison. It's also triumphant in tone. 'Bubbles' is about futility and West Ham are capable of blowing more than bubbles; they often blow chances.

West Ham go into today's game as underdogs in the same manner as against Arsenal in 1980. I was only four then but my sense of occasion was refined enough to recognise the significance of that day. When Second Division (as was then) West Ham faced the mighty Arsenal, even as a tot, Willy Young's boorish challenge on the adolescent Paul Allen made me wince and how my young heart soared when Sir Trevor's O-level-stuffed head vanquished the Gunners. That victory was achieved under the management of John Lyall, whereas West Ham's previous Cup wins came in 1964 under Ron Greenwood and 1975 under the pair of them. Both have died during our journey to Cardiff.

I was present at both the games that immediately followed their deaths. At each game the tributes to these gentle patriarchs were unusual. At Villa Park, aside from Marlon Harewood's goal, the most exhilarating moment came before kick-off when, during Lyall's minute's silence, a solitary and bold voice sang out 'Johnny Lyall's Claret and Blue army'. Now, the protocols of silences are unanimously accepted and rigorously enforced, and those that breach the silence do so at their peril. For a moment, Villa Park held its breath, before, as one, the West Ham faithful decreed that this transgression was a far more fitting testimony than silence and joined the chant and once more his army marched. Risky, though, for that first bloke takes a lot of confidence. What if everyone had just rolled their eyes and tutted? I've never had the bottle to start a chant and I bristle with heterosexual admiration for those to whom it's but a trifle, the generals of the Claret and Blue army.

Greenwood's minute's silence took place at Upton Park when we hosted Birmingham. I was with my mate Ade, who's in a wheelchair. So we were right at the front of the Centenary Stand. Sir Trevor came out to begin proceedings and the silence was, as they say, immaculately observed. I reflected on how beautiful it was: 34,000 people in that moment putting aside their personal concerns in a unified show of respect. Alan Pardew indicated that it was West Ham's destiny to win the Cup this year for Ron Greenwood and John Lyall.

That would be magical, romantic, perfect. Only Liverpool stand in the way. The pragmatic might of walking through storms with 'your head held high' versus a whimsical devotion to 'pretty bubbles' . . . I think West Ham will win the FA Cup today.

World Cup: Oh, for a vulgar ending to chapter '06

10 June 2006

Beyond the saccharine nostalgia and the sanctioned xenophobia there is a unifying truth that visits us at four-year intervals that somehow remains untainted by the ubiquitous wallcharts, the oscillation between glee and panic over the progress of that year's injured talisman, and even the grotesque appearance of the trophy at the tournament's zenith. The World Cup in its grandeur and infrequency provides all of Earth's citizens with shared chapter headings for our lives right across the globe.

My first World Cup was Mexico '86. (My Spain '82 can be condensed into the mascot: the orange with legs, Paolo Rossi, Kevin Keegan carrying an injury, coming on and ballsing up a header by being flash, and Harald Schumacher's foul on that French substitute.) I was 10 years old in '86 and crap at football, a shameful admission for any man, amplified by the fact that both my dad and stepdad were, at different times, favourably eyed by West Ham scouts. Prepubescently, an inability to kick a ball was akin to having a My Little Pony in lieu of testicles.

To this day I endure a bilious dread when a wayward ball rolls towards me in a park. 'Someone else get it,' I think, or else I ignore the cries to return it. On the occasions when I've obliged I've always hoofed it skyward or spooned it in a lake or a pensioner's lap. My dad joyfully floats the ball back having flicked it about a bit to present his credentials.

Despite this embarrassing inability, in '86 I still felt part of the World Cup, enthralled by the Mexican Wave and the partnership of Gary Lineker and Peter Beardsley. Lineker had an injured wrist, which was bandaged during the tournament. I faithfully recreated this attainable attribute of the tanned and gleaming deity with a bandage of my own as I wheezed and stumbled after a plastic ball on the rec with Topsy, my dog, guesting as Paraguay. I think perhaps she won. Bryan Robson, that year's injured talisman, didn't excite me in the same way as Lineker, though. Naturally I was horrified by his shoulder injury and I recall too the very English sense of moral condemnation attached to Ray Wilkins's sending off.

But Mexico '86 did not belong to England or Lineker, despite his six goals and Golden Boot. It was of course Diego Maradona's World Cup. By divine right, by holy ability, by the hand of God. I hated him. The awed sense of injustice that moment engendered has since been tempered by an appreciation of Maradona's genius and an awareness of the context provided by the Falklands conflict, but at the time the confusion and indignation were unmanageable. He can't do that, can he? The second goal was irrelevant. He cheated, that's not allowed. Nobody could explain what had happened and why, because the bafflement I felt as a 10-year-old appeared to be a national affliction.

The next day Jamie Dawkins, the hardest kid at our school, told me the match was to be replayed. I believed him, not just because questioning his word was punishable by death but because it seemed right. I have often wondered what motivated Dawkins to lie. I shudder to remember him. He was only 10 but he had the demeanour of Vinnie Jones and seemed constantly to be on the precipice of casual violence. He was harder than the lads in the year above us and the girls loved him (why is that?) and although he lacked skill as a footballer his menace was a licence to patrol the field, ball at his feet, fists clenched, goal-bound, triumph inevitable. Even he felt castrated by Maradona's sleight of hand. Jamie Dawkins, impervious to the authority of the most draconian dinner ladies, was as broken and powerless as the rest of us.

Italia '90 was Platt's goal, Gazza's tears and penalties. '94, no qualification and it was in America anyway which was an unsettling anomaly. By '98 I had progressed from chubby child to wretched drug addict but through the haze I could still taste the injustice, savour Michael Owen, detest David Beckham and, once more, loathe Argentina. '02 was daft. Matches in the morning, two hosts and a foreign coach. It all seemed odd, a sense heightened by the fact I was addicted to heroin and watching matches at 7am, boozing in a Leeds pub with the young BNP (I was making a documentary, I'm not a racist).

So Germany '06. What'll it be? Battling with the hosts? Further disputes and friction with the Argies? Or will our injured man-child deliver us from evil? Be nice to win the ol' World Cup. Be nice to see Cap'n Becks lift that vulgar lump of gold. Be nice if '06's chapter became Rooney, Germany, our second World Cup.

World Cup: In bed or watching it in the pub – it pays to keep your mouth shut

17 June 2006

The World Cup is now all around us, it is the context in which we exist. For me it feels like a hard-won romantic conquest where the actualisation of that which we have strived to attain can be baffling and irreconcilable with expectation.

Saturday's game against Paraguay I watched at a mate's house. I think in the group stages it's acceptable to spectate in a smaller, more intimate setting before being inevitably, inertly poured into the fizzing hive of communal viewing of the knock-out stage.

I love going to football, mostly Upton Park, where I first experienced the awareness of divinity and awe when I ascended the stairs of the East Stand as was, aged seven, and beheld the expanse of the pitch and after the match looked out on to the Green Street exodus, overwhelmed by the multitudes – 'Is that all the people in the world, Dad?' I like watching it on telly an' all or with a few friends – the communal pub watching is what I struggle with.

In 2002 I was making a documentary about the young BNP and watched the Argentina game with them – very patriotic, them lads. I also recall the jarringly homoerotic kisses they shared in celebration of David Beckham's goal which sat uncomfortably with their ill-informed views about gays, charmingly dubbed 'AIDs monkeys' by Mark Collett, who is doing quite well in the BNP these days and is standing for a council seat.

I don't drink any more, so I don't have a local and pubs are anathema to me now – the jostling jocundity present at screened matches unsettles me.

My self-consciousness in these situations was compounded when, during Portugal '04, a girl told me that my celebration of Wayne Rooney's second goal looked awkward. Shouting at a football match, like talking during sex, should only be undertaken with supreme confidence and commitment.

Yelping, 'Blimey, you've done a goal' or 'I'm gonna do a sex on you' can mar, irrevocably, the necessary tension. Also, the sense of togetherness and unity that occurs so organically in the World Cup, which always seems contrived during the Olympics, can be undermined if you find yourself dreaming the same dream as an obnoxious goon or braying twerp. Yes, we're all in this together. But I don't want to be in this together with you – I'd rather be in this together alone.

The second game, too, I watched in near solitude. I loathe ITV coverage. The BBC is what football should sound like and Sky are at least professional. Clive Tyldesley and Gareth Southgate just slung inconsequential clichés around for 90 minutes, perpetually perplexed by the physicality of Peter Crouch.

Though, if I may, I'll contribute to that debate: Crouch, even in name, seems like a Victorian oddity – 'Igor, fetch "the Crouch" from the catacombs, we're going to the graveyard.'

Roman battalions kept an elephant among their ranks, not because they contributed much from a military perspective, but because of the gawping delirium this berserk addition to the artillery would evoke in opponents. And to witness the affable gangle-tang of limbs sans gorm must at least bemuse our foes.

What a delightful double act he and Rooney made in the second half against Trinidad & Tobago. Rooney's porcine squint bristling with bound devastation like febrile livestock, a rosette-spattered minotaur so brimming with force that when denied action, he's a danger to his team-mates and himself.

It's easy to imagine this destructive, Kali-like energy leading young Wayne into the crimson-lipped arms of a snaggle-toothed matriarch just to grunt and vent his darkly beautiful potency.

We can't ignore the lacklustre nature of these first two ventures but my heart has made its mind up and I've decided to remain cock-eyed. If Steven Gerrard plays less deep, if Aaron Lennon starts, if Frank Lampard has his foot recalibrated (like that bit in *Robocop* where his pistol is realigned), if Michael Owen, front of the class, neat parting, little boffin of mercurial tics and kicks gets over his writer's block, then I maintain we can triumph.

Italy look efficient, Tomas Rosicky and the Republic are exciting, Spain have turned up, the Germans are the Germans and Brazil remain Brazil. But Albion must be hopeful: John Terry, from the quill of Siegfried Sassoon, is full of lethal pride and Beckham is still golden. These things I hold to be true but I'd never shout them in a crowded London pub, or during copulation for that matter.

World Cup: It's necessity and dread time for England

24 June 2006

Right, I'll tell you how I'm going to maintain my optimism, despite England's second-half collapse against Sweden: conceding clumsily, needlessly. Despite Argentina's breath-taking performance against Serbia & Montenegro, Brazil's continued revival and the integrity of oft-slumbering nations such as Holland, Spain and Italy.

Disregarding the indisputable aforementioned, I shall comfort myself thusly: I have all week to write this column on any facet of the tournament that I choose. Usually, I focus on my reaction to England matches. They played Sweden on Tuesday night, so I could have begun writing after the game and had it finished for Wednesday. Night fell on Wednesday, however, without a single word having been written and Thursday too passed without travail. Only on Friday with my face flattened against the deadline did I, adrenalised and flushed, scratch my frantic opinions on to the page with the twisted lust of a self-harming adolescent etching anxious, doubtful journals upon her busy wrists.

Perhaps now the knockout stage has begun, and Germany have been avoided, England can begin. Perhaps necessity and dread will trigger – like my deadline – heretofore absent skill and fluency because three games in it still seems as if the tournament has yet to begin for Blighty.

Aside from Joe Cole's goal on Tuesday and Steven Gerrard's against Trinidad & Tobago there has been little to stir the loins. In the first half against Sweden there were moments on the left when Cole justified the bluster and guff, since eclipsed by the sparkle-eyed sasquatch from Merseyside, that commenced with puberty and caused Sir Alex to inquire after his progress like an aged suitor willing the ripening of teenage prey.

It's a bloody good job that goals are coming from midfield now that Michael Owen has chuckled his way back to Toon. He was giggling on those crutches when surely he must be devastated, not least because he's regarded as a kind of Kunte Kinte by the Prince Philip of the Premiership, Freddy Shepherd. 'When you lend someone something and they break it, you expect them to pay for it to be mended.'

One suspects that Owen is finished now, that his goal against Argentina in '98 was his zenith, the asphyxiating euphoria we felt retrospectively validated as we were witnessing a premature swansong, like Orson Welles arriving with Citizen Kane, an altitude seldom visited twice. So Shepherd reducing him to the status of a loaned record-player is boorish in extremis.

Odd injury though, to have sustained cruciate ligament damage while stood alone on the flank seconds after kick-off. It seemed arbitrary that it occurred then and abstract from the game. I fear it may become a moment that defines our progress, an excuse for failings yet to come. 'We lost Rooney against Portugal' and 'Beckham wasn't fit against Brazil' having been offered as mitigation for departure in the two previous competitions. Rooney is at least keen. Even were he not so sublimely blessed, his touchingly apparent frustration mirrors the fans' and he has a crackling authenticity no amount of media training can emolliate. If he carried Max Clifford around in a knapsack relentlessly muttering into his constantly incarnadine lughole he'd still eff and blind and lash out at dugouts.

How many pairs of boots did he remove on Tuesday? Every time the camera cut back to him he was petulantly tossing aside another. Was Sammy Lee, like an obsessive-compulsive blacksmith, re-shoeing him to prolong the outburst? It went on interminably. 'There's Rooney throwing down his boots in disgust.' It was like a tantrum from a centipede.

Rooney's ability alone could drag us into the quarter-finals, but I fear his shoe-chucking, bench-punching passion could be misdirected and cause injury or cards. It seems that genius, even when not academic or artistic, has stitched into its fabric this element of self-destruction and this must be contained. Paul Gascoigne once spoke of walking with his mother when he was seven and suddenly becoming aware that one day she'd die and it provoked an anxiety in him that has never departed.

It is an anecdote one would expect to hear from Brendan Behan, Tracey Emin or Richard Dawkins; this painful awareness of mortality is ill at ease with the tongue-wagging, gurning clown that we so adore. But I suppose there's no real paradox, he's just a regular genius.

As yet we cannot discern the value of Theo Walcott for the simple reason that Sven seems unwilling to play him. The decision to go to Germany bereft of Bent and Defoe seems increasingly eccentric. Personal feelings (as a West Ham fan) for the latter aside, he is as close to a replacement for Owen as we have and it would be heartening to have him now.

Walcott, one can only assume, must be good company, a laugh to have about the camp, a dab hand at close-up magic or a spinner of incredible yarns, cos he don't appear to be there for the football.

World Cup: Let teary pain turn to bongo-playing joy

1 July 2006

I suppose the quarter-finals is the minimum I expect as an Englishman. Were this column to be an obituary, lamenting defeat by Ecuador, I would feel swindled. Deprived of the routine despondence of a quarter-final exit from the World Cup would make me feel incomplete. When we get to the semis, where the adjacent thrill of the final throbs in your tum, the vertigo near unmanageable, it's almost a triumph of its own. But for us quarter-finals are defining.

Today, as is often the case, is the first time we face a decent team. Portugal, of course, knocked us out of our last major tournament at the quarter-final stage, and by this evening the ubiquitous bunting and flags may listlessly hang – tattered and unwelcome mementoes of a shared dream, abruptly ended like broken mirrors in a ghost town. They'll cast long shadows, these endless flags, should we not win the World Cup, like cherished love tokens that spear your heart when the spell inevitably breaks.

I think we ought to beat the Portuguese; they'll miss Deco,

a charming player. The image of him and his Barcelona team-mate Giovanni van Bronckhorst, sat with glum, curdled acceptance after both were dismissed in Portugal's second-round tie against Holland, was a moment that captured the unity that frames this competition. A tableau of all that is beautiful in World Cup football.

I fear Portugal, stymied though they are by the lack of Deco and Costinha, for one reason: Luiz Felipe Scolari. As Pauleta portentously observed yesterday, there is little between the teams in ability but Portugal have a manager, a coach, a leader who can make adjustments in the heat of battle. Can England say the same? One can see why Scolari was so thirstily courted by the FA. He exudes potency, and though aesthetically he lacks a single beautiful feature, he has attractive obvious authority and charisma.

I don't want to harp on like a gigglesome *Heat* devotee about 'magnetism' and 'fellows' but the man has qualities that inspire admiration. He is bold where Sven is insipid, confident where Sven is meek. I imagine that after victories 'Big' Phil strides, nude, into the team bath and embraces his charges, guffawing and proud as the gleeful players unwittingly release inadvertent spurts of grateful widdle.

Sven, I expect, enacts some nutless shuffle from tunnel to limo perhaps issuing handshakes to the more senior players. I bet he wears pants in the bath.

The tangible passion that Scolari exhibits during his touchline celebrations and war dances is present in his current side. Latin and South American teams play football. Play. It's a game. England work football. The first four games have been largely joyless. Snatches from Cole, Rooney, Gerrard and Lennon appear as lapses in the current dogma.

Should Portugal be defeated, Scolari's former team most likely await us for a fraught semi-final, another opponent that issued a quarter-final execution. My friend Helen is Brazilian and has just returned from a visit to her homeland where she spoke of the intrinsic relationship between football and music. The World Cup in Brazil sounds like an alien experience to one who looks on from a teary Saxon perspective.

There are similarities – like in Blighty, the streets are awash in national livery and the country all but stops during games – but in Brazil the shared experience is one of joy. Here in England we endure an anxious carnival of pain, a Mardi Gras of malcontent, a samba of sadness. Christ, when they have their opulent decadent Fat Tuesday (literally Mardi Gras) we have Pancake Day. They shag in the streets while we squeeze out Jif lemon on to fried apologetic slop.

When Brazil travel to matches Ronaldinho plays bongos and the lads share in frenzied just optimism. I saw Michael Carrick interviewed with headphones around his neck and I imagined he, Beckham and Ferdinand solipsistically locked into iPod isolation, nailed to the beats of Jay Z or Dizzy.

During the 80s with Liverpool's European dominance, though they had only a smattering of Englishmen, I suppose our innately militaristic nation tasted victory. It happened once more with United and one suspects that Chelsea may now achieve great things in Europe. But I'm a West Ham fan and an Englishman and witness victory from afar, blinking at the distant glisten and wondering when. When Sven? Perhaps today. Let's say today.

World Cup: If defeat is our destiny, I need a divorce

8 July 2006

This time when it happened I vowed to divorce myself from emotion, to untether the fortunes of our hapless nation from my heart. The macabre ritual we endure, the cyclical cruelty of the narrative. When Portugal celebrated in ecstatic Latin exuberance I tried to steel myself in static indifference but silently urged the camera to stray from their carnival. But where could it linger, the suddenly intrusive eye? On the maudlin, slumped, stringless marionettes stripped of platitudes, cloaked only in failure? It seems to me in this tableau we witnessed the actualisation of the innate qualities of two nations, that this gloomy defeat was ever England's destiny, that Portugal had been raised to conquer.

Now all that's left is the futile allocation of blame with two obvious contenders having emerged as potential targets for disproportionate antipathy. Firstly Cristiano Ronaldo, dubbed the 'winker' by the tabloids having apparently issued a conspiratorial wink after his cajoling perhaps ensured Wayne Rooney's dismissal. Not really satisfying as a scapegoat – though I am sure he will be whooped out of Blighty by seething red tops.

Interestingly there doesn't seem to be an appetite to vilify Rooney himself. One tabloid ran the headline '10 lions and one donkey' which is, of course, a retread of the banner which followed David Beckham's red card in 1998.

That headline's inaugural usage was much more in keeping with the national sentiment but I fancy there will be no effigies of Rooney hung outside south London boozers which is perhaps a blessing because their manufacture might necessitate grave robbing. I suppose this is because as a signifier he represents much more than just the talented footballer that Beckham did.

But while Beckham's sending-off was preceded by the hairdos, sarongs, celebrity girlfriend and obvious narcissism, Rooney has been hewn from English rock truly representative of the aspirations of the fans – the way Steven Gerrard is for Liverpool.

Beckham's prostrate girlish lash was indicative of his image at that time, similarly Rooney's frustrated goolie stamp appears symptomatic of his frustration at having been left adrift upfront. You can't condemn Wayne because I think at that point all England ached to administer a righteous stamp to the spunkless stones of the true villain of this tragedy – Sven-Goran Eriksson.

There was a moment amid the numb aftermath of defeat where he offered comfort to Peter Crouch who had played admirably after his forced substitution, holding the ball up so well that had he been simultaneously present with Rooney the latter's frustration could have been assuaged and his sending-off avoided.

Eriksson presented an awkward withered arm of consolation to Crouch, like an uneasy stepfather to a detested child. Attempting to quell another failed Christmas. Crouch just looked embarrassed. Mind you, he never looks that comfortable; he looks like playing football hurts him – mewling and gasping.

Nor did I much care for his speech where he urged us not to 'kill' Rooney. It seemed to me like Mark Antony reassuring Rome that Brutus 'is an honourable man'. Eriksson's words appeared to be designed to divert blame from himself and nominate young Wayne for national backlash and culpability.

Sven is like a Nordic Uriah Heep: 'Don't blame Rooney, it would be ever so awful if you done him in, though it were him that got sent awf – I'm much too 'umble to take responsibility for ineffective tactics and poor team selection.'

There's no point harping on about tactics and selection, we just have to brace ourselves and march onwards, without even the satisfaction of seeing him sacked. And his apprentice don't inspire much hope either – Steve

McClaren has been present throughout this drab catastrophe, blushing in his shorts like a suspect PE teacher dogged by vicious rumour.

The moment Lampard stepped up for the first kick one heard the distant knell with which someone should have stopped him: 'It's not your night Frank, sit this one out. Let me get a cow's arse and a banjo – let's do this one step at a time.' Gerrard's miss was eviscerating, the only person who scored was Hargreaves and as one exasperated Radio 5 caller pointed out 'that's because he's German'.

Like a fledgling tainted by human hands, we found it so hard to accept him but it was Hargreaves who most impressed in the quarter-final – relentless, focused and bold. The rest of 'em – content to audition for future Pizza Hut commercials – drove me to make untenable pledges: to boycott Nando's, to follow Wimbledon and, most importantly, never again to be seduced by the three lions, and hopeless impotent optimism. But, of course, I said that last time.

Bog-standard banter proved my fan credentials

16 September 2006

Curse these cynical times in which we live – an age when West Ham United can't even purchase two of the world's finest South American players without other clubs looking on covetously with suspicious eyes, alleging that the Boleyn is merely a shop front for Chelsea and that soon oligarchal claws will be clutching at the shoulders of Carlos Tevez and nape of Javier Mascherano, and swooping across London.

Well, know you this: I saw Tevez march on to the pitch against Aston Villa and he played with a commitment and dedication of a man who will be there for decades. I predict he'll be an Argentinian Billy Bonds. I'm confident that Tevez will remain at West Ham into his dotage then become Alan Pardew's assistant and perhaps, even when his playing career is finally over, when he is but a gurgling shipwreck of a man, he will become one of the Hammers' seemingly endless irritating mascots, joining that hammer and daft cat-thing people are forced to tolerate that put me off the half-time enjoyment of The Hammerettes – God bless them girls.

There's an anxious vigour about the side since the arrival of these footballing gigolos, these Johnny-come-lately saviours of the club. I only hope it doesn't unsettle Bobby Zamora, crocked Dean Ashton and Hayden Mullins. Marlon Harewood played the first half like a tentative mutt on its final journey to an indifferent vet.

The game against Villa was the first I've attended at Upton Park this season. When I arrived I was happily scribbling autographs, posing for photographs and, a joy I never thought I'd experience, signing West Ham shirts for children – a man of my desperately limited football talents really has no right defacing the Claret and Blue strip.

At half-time I made the mistake of using the lavatory in the Dr Martens Stand unaccompanied. Further autographs and photographs ensued. This caught the attention of a group of what I can only describe as lads. Or possibly yobs. As they queued to buy drinks, I became the focus of their good-natured chants beginning with: 'Who the fucking hell are you?' Moving on to: 'Brandy is a wanker.' Followed by a burst of: 'Sex case, sex case, 'ang 'im, 'ang 'im, 'ang 'im.' Borrowed from the film *McVicar.* High jinks, yes, but unnerving none the less. And then: 'Where were you when we were shit?'

'Well frankly,' I internally remarked, 'we were shit in the first half, I was in my seat watching us being shit.' But of course they meant where were you in previous, less successful seasons. To which I would like to rather belatedly respond. I was here but you didn't recognise me because I didn't have a famous hairdo. Obviously I didn't have the confidence to articulate that at the time because I was too busy maintaining control of both my frontal and rear sphincters. The tone of these taunts was essentially garrulous, ribald tormenting as opposed to an aggressive onslaught. Blessedly I was given a chance to redeem myself.

'Brandy, give us a song . . .' (Brandy? I never thought the day would come where I'd be dubbed Brandy by a terrace choir), 'Brandy, Brandy, give us a song.'

I knew this was not a moment in which to be inhibited, I had to commit 100 per cent or be considered a fraud, a fair-weather fan, like Lennox Lewis screaming 'come on you Irons' in a Canadian accent. The worst accusation one could endure. Thankfully, in spite of having no ability to kick a ball, and having none of the traits one would typically associate with a football supporter, I am a lifelong West Ham fan and have a broad repertoire of songs to draw from. I opted not for the obvious 'I'm Forever Blowing Bubbles' because that wouldn't have been sufficient testimony to my commitment. I steeled myself, flung my arms skyward and retreated into the accent of my childhood. Going at least three octaves lower than my natural speaking voice I bellowed: 'We all follow the West Ham over land and sea . . .'

I could see the eyes of the tribe soften as they saw my fidelity to the lyrics of that song. By the time I got to '. . . all together now', which I believe is the middle eight of the chant, me and the lads chimed out in unison a glorious chorus of 'We all follow the West Ham on to victory . . .'

Many ran to congratulate and hug me. I was accepted. One, to show his acceptance (I don't know what manner of ritual this is), tipped some beer on my head. I've never felt more loved. Then, before I reached the lavatory, Zamora equalised, chaos erupted and I was swept off my feet. Embraced. More beer sloshed about on to my, retrospectively, ill-advised footwear – the flip-flop. Thankfully, again, I was equipped with the appropriate ditty. To the tune of Dean Martin's 'Volare', 'Zamora ooh-ooh, Zamora ooh-ooh/He came from Shite Hart Lane/He's better than Jermain . . .'

With that rendered I was free to attend the urinal, only troubled by a gentleman who wanted to take a photo of my genitals. I returned to my seat drenched in beer, but with a new-found sense of belonging. In spite of an unremarkable result this occasion will live in my memory as the day that West Ham became a club that could house the world's finest talent and where one of digital television's campest men could lead a joyful battle hymn.

The significance of this event will remain with all present. Perhaps I will be commemorated at Upton Park with a statue or maybe they'll rename the North Bank The Randy Brandy Standy.

Not waving but drowning in a sea of bile

23 September 2006

I hope to God that Sam Allardyce is innocent. I've always regarded him as a sort of ebullient, avuncular greengrocer. And I hope that in time we'll see that he ain't been mis-handling his sprouts. I haven't seen the footage but it's the kind of accusation that, once made, immediately taints. I hope the Allardyce name, already laden with syllables, doesn't have to carry the further burden of alleged murky dealings.

It will be a long time before the name of Glenn Roeder is uttered in east London without the accompaniment of flecks of bile. I was present for his return to Upton Park with Newcastle. The seething anticipation of this event had been slightly muted by the arrival of Javier Mascherano and Carlos Tevez.

Roeder escaped recrimination due to the nature of his departure – he, of course, had a brain tumour and was desperately ill. Before it was diagnosed Roeder was despised for his ineffective stewardship at the helm of the Hammers.

Approaching the end of his reign when losing at home to Leeds, I recall a grim knell from the terrace – 'Roeder, you've killed West Ham'.

He was extended sympathy due to his deteriorating health and it seemed inappropriate to say, 'How could you sell Paolo Di Canio? What were you thinking, man?', when he was teetering on the precipice of death. Bill Shankly's maxim – 'Football is not a matter of life and death; it's far more important than that' – seems quite trite in the face of actual mortality.

West Ham once more seemed a little drab and directionless to me. It seems that the glamorous recent arrivals have upset the domestic balance of the side like J-Lo and Angelina Jolie tottering into an Essex discotheque.

Sunday's game was only enlivened when, at the behest of the unbelievably effervescent Toon Army, Roeder waved. 'Roeder, give us a wave. Roeder, Roeder give us a wave.' Roeder gave them a wave. Once the wave was made, he was drowning, not waving, in a sea of acrimony, antipathy, and abuse. It was an unwise wave. When the home crowd had made clear their disapproval, he waved twice more.

It's intriguing to be a part of a crowd in a moment like that. West Ham had been lacklustre, they were 2-0 down, uninspiring to watch but suddenly Roeder made himself the focus of hate, and the game lived again. The agitated home support groped for a response, some fled all the way from behind the goal to the dugout and had to be apprehended by the police.

Others began to chant: 'You're the reason we went down.' Soon the ground fizzed with this mantra, angry rhythmic fists pointing in Roeder's direction. What must it feel like to be the focus of such discontent, of such disdain? He is, as I recall, a sensitive man and to feel such audacious wrath must be blood-curdling. I know myself when I have been booed on stage, I still hear the jeering crowd as my head settles on my pillow.

How he was able to embrace Mrs Roeder that night is a mystery to me. Every conjugal stroke greeted with a sneer or hateful cry. I was torn in this moment naturally I was caught up in the gleeful hysteria of the mob. I found myself busily searching my mind for a witty rhyme that might become an instant terrace hit. Is it morally acceptable to compose a ditty using the word tumour? Fortunately the moment passed before I could commit an atrocity of that nature.

Last week I described how on a half-time visit to the toilet I was cajoled into singing to appease a braying lad flock. Thankfully someone recorded the excruciating episode on their mobile phone and put it on youtube.com, so should you wish to witness the incident you can.

It's interesting how one behaves when part of a crowd, the diminished responsibility, the intoxicating fervour. As one of thousands I'm quite content to convey insensitive, incendiary sentiments to an apparently sweet man, whose only crime was to be crap at his job. Would I be happy to express these views on a one to one basis? Would I scream into the face of an inefficient post office clerk 'I hope you get cancer' if I knew that at the time they were undergoing chemotherapy?

After the game I went to the players' lounge, an environment that makes me chuckle and swoon like a Bros-ette, trying to catch Anton Ferdinand's eye by coquettishly applying lipstick and pushing out my cleavage. I made a trip to the lavvy to powder my nose and flung open the door to reveal Roeder doing up his fly.

I was struck by the bruised humanity of the man, a man who only half an hour before had inspired me to ransack my brain to conjure a jingoistic ditty to belittle a serious illness that he'd endured. Although I didn't shake his hand – he had after all just been to the toilet – upon seeing the vulnerability in his eyes I certainly didn't think to myself, hmmm . . . I wonder what rhymes with haemorrhage.

Che's clarion call to the Boleyn: on your feet, lads

30 September 2006

I shan't harp on about the negativity inherent in the lyric 'Then like my dreams they fade and die' because it's something I've pondered in this column before. But after West Ham's defeat in Sicily, the lachrymose sentimentality of the song 'Bubbles' seems, once more, apposite.

This inaugural match of our 'European Tour' sent a frisson through the claret-and-blue army. When the final whistle blew at the FA Cup final in Cardiff, West Ham's last-minute defeat against Liverpool was quickly absorbed and fans immediately consoled each other with dreams of the forthcoming Uefa adventure.

Palermo, West Ham's first and only opponents, have stitched deep into their culture links with Cosa Nostra – a fact that evoked jocular torment for their visit to the Boleyn, with Godfather 'marionette' T-shirts being sold around the ground. West Ham also have an insular and familial tradition, and geographically the club is ensconced in our capital's own petit gangland. Ronnie and Reggie Kray borrowed heavily from Mafia symbology with their dapper suits, their insistence on loyalty and their devotion to their ol' mom who went to her grave thinking her boys were a couple of angels.

I didn't travel to Sicily for the match but I called my mate Neil who was there. He said the atmosphere was hostile and he had been among a group of fans who'd endured a hail of bricks and slate hurled by the angry townsfolk, emerging from catacombs and alleys and looming off of scaffolds. As is often the case with these reports, it seems the police were primed to make arrests and that the locals anticipated hostility.

Of course my friend is a lovely fella, but I think only the naive would deny that in the midst of West Ham's well behaved fraternity are a few 'Herberts' whom it must be disconcerting to see romping across a beloved plaza, emanating impotent rage and belittling organised crime.

It was a fixture that always had the potential to spawn brouhaha: the pride at returning to European competition seemed to have an odd-yet-intrinsic connection to friction. Unlike a lot of Premiership clubs, particularly in the capital, West Ham has maintained contact with its original fan base of white working-class men: decent, honest, passionate and brave men for whom a sense of disenfranchisement has been incrementally consuming their territory and culture since the '60s, and the terraces and their team are perhaps the last front left to fight for.

I spoke to a bloke called Andy who sits near me and has begun a campaign to entitle fans to stand in certain areas of the ground (standupsitdown.co.uk). In talking to him it became apparent that being forced to sit is emasculating, a further castration in an environment that traditionally was exempt from such restrictions. It's interesting to me that this situation has politicised Andy.

Roy Keane famously bemoaned the culture of prawn sandwiches and indifferent fans in executive boxes. The constant renewal of strips, the spiralling ticket prices are expenses faithfully tolerated by football's hardcore support, but being forced to remain sedentary, it seems, is one restriction too many.

Che Guevara said: 'I'd rather die on my feet than live on my knees.' This clarion call is heard once more across East London from the mountains of the Sierra Maestra all the way to the Boleyn Ground the thirst for liberty remains unquenched. Be it from Cuban rebels or cockney devotees, the message is the same – we will remain on our feet.

The atmosphere at matches has undoubtedly suffered since all-seater stadiums became *de rigueur*, but this is something most people were prepared to accept after Hillsborough and the Taylor Report. To some, though, this erosion of freedom is unpalatable.

'Stand up if you love West Ham, Stand up if you love West Ham' is a frequent chant and, when momentum is sufficient, it's a great joy to answer this cry by climbing to your feet, arms aloft. But often the chant is a murmur and one feels self-conscious – 'What if I'm the only one who stands?' you think. It seems to me that for some, when they rise they are not only standing up for a love of West Ham but also for a culture that could be lost in a Blue ocean of foreign cash and corporate values cascading from the west.

Palermo fans on Thursday night hummed the Godfather theme before their side drubbed the luckless Hammers, and in so doing they reclaimed control of a tool that in the previous leg had been used to berate them. I wonder if the fading legacy that underscores our game will continue to ring out, or if that too will fade and die.

It's yesterday once more with old father Tel

7 October 2006

As an English West Ham supporter I feel like my resources of optimism are relentlessly plundered and that I can no longer remain cock-eyed. How are we as a nation, less than four months after our departure from the World Cup in Germany, to conjure the goodwill and belief required to enjoy this match against Macedonia? Steve McClaren was after all present throughout Sven-Goran Eriksson's reign. It's difficult to herald a new dawn when it so tangibly smacks of yesterday.

And equally odd is that McClaren has chosen to emerge from Eriksson's shadow arm-in-arm with the spiv-duke of Dagenham, Terry Venables. The choice of Venables as his No2 is a popular one. Everyone I've spoken to thinks it's a great decision. Venables as a man elicits great warmth from people, me included. I think of him as a kind of sexy Father Christmas. There are few men upon whose laps I'd happily sit without feeling compromised. I can think of nothing more comforting than to curl up on the thighs of El Tel, sedated by the Aramis whiff and slurp egg-nog from a baby bottle – I assume all Englishmen feel the same.

I think the decision to appoint Venables has been inspired by nostalgia. I approve of this because I'm a nostalgic man – when I think of the achievements of Euro 96, how close we came to the final, it's easy for me to become lachrymose and sentimental. Why stop at Venables, why not play Steve McManaman in midfield? Why not bring back Gazza and Alan Shearer? Why don't we resurrect the Twin Towers and stand smothered in rosettes twirling rattles in our hands, guzzling pies, defiant against the Hun, shoulder to shoulder behind our brave boys?

Euro 96 was a fabulous tournament. I was living above a pub in north London, working shifts in lieu of rent. When England went out on penalties, I was working behind the bar, drunk and disillusioned. My friends who also lived in the pub had watched the game elsewhere and my way of coping with yet another English defeat was to joke about it, saying something mock-conciliatory like: 'Don't worry, in a decade's time Terry Venables will return under the stewardship of Steve McClaren. A man whose gin-blossoming schnoz is morphing by the day into that of the Knight of Old Trafford. Mourn not for the loss of Venables, for a decade from now he'll come wheezing back to the fore.' This I did foresee with the perspicacity of a tipsy Nostradamus.

Venables now, great manager though he may have been, is quite old. Isn't he rather old for that kind of responsibility? There are members of my family less aged than him who I wouldn't trust to organise my sock drawer, let alone the England defence.

So today against Macedonia will it be 3-5-2 or 4-4-2? It looks like Shaun Wright-Phillips might play, which would mean that Ian Wright's punditry will again be hugely biased. What about that time when Wright-Phillips was substituted, Wright refused to join in on the post-match commentary. I admire Wright's authenticity and honesty. Perhaps he should also be brought into the management structure and we could work on subdividing Wright-Phillips to play in every position. England, I'm sure, will beat Macedonia today but will we recapture the heady days of Euro 96? Gazza's flick, Shearer's glint, Pearce's war cry. I imagine the answer is no.

I'm in no position to debunk nostalgia – if it were up to me World Cup coins would replace the pound – but it worries me when a national team needing desperately to move forward starts to ransack the past. The set-up of the England coaching staff feels like the British Museum with stolen Elgin Marbles and artefacts from around the globe, monuments from yesteryear propping up the structure of our national team. It's difficult to worry about whether Michael Carrick or Scott Parker should replace the injured Owen Hargreaves when it seems that any minute Alf Ramsey might be summoned from the spirit world to offer tactical advice. I hope to God the top brass at the FA have not been watching *The Match* on Sky One or it may herald the return of Graham Taylor to the hierarchy.

Perhaps England should follow the example of *The Match* and field a team of preening celebrities against Macedonia, then I might get a game and my enthusiasm might be truly stoked. Even if England do win and eventually qualify for the European Championship, where will it lead to? One can't help but think, to more disappointment.

At least Venables' involvement means that when England's inevitable failure arrives we can sit and watch episodes of his self-penned cop drama *Hazell* in a private booth at his nightclub Scribes, snug in a blanket of cosy nostalgia.

McClaren is a master tactician . . . oh no, he isn't!

14 October 2006

The weather may be almost supernaturally warm, giving the impression that Jack Frost's icy digits can be kept at bay, but in the world of international football the pantomime season has evidently begun.

The performances against Macedonia and Croatia contained so much slapstick goonery that it would not have been visually jarring to see Harold Lloyd and Buster Keaton at the heart of England's defence – and Fatty Arbuckle would have been an advantage between the sticks. Watching the usually impeccable John Terry play at international level is like being forced to endure the spectacle of Marlon Brando playing Widow Twankey in an amateur dramatic production of *Aladdin*.

'It's behind you, John,' yelled the mob, and the 'it' in question was Paul Robinson, thrashing wildly at the air like someone being pursued by an imaginary bee. Confounded by a divot, this being a word that will enter the public consciousness much as Florida's 'hanging chads' did in the infamous presidential election of 2000, or 'metatarsal' did when David Beckham, then Wayne Rooney, broke one.

Since Wednesday I think of naught but divots. 'Oh, we've been defeated by a divot.' Perhaps now England should field a team of 11 divots and, given a chance to represent our unduly proud nation, I fancy that the divots will be grateful for the opportunity and will provoke less scandal. Before long we will see razor blades and pizzas endorsed by millionaire divots.

Alas, when performing for England, the reverse alchemy of the three lions on their chest seems to be turning golden club players into base-metal internationals.

Admittedly, for this performance we were without Steven Gerrard, Joe Cole and the ever-electrifying Aaron Lennon. It seems impertinent to already be thinking, 'Oh, perhaps Theo Walcott will save us,' like a pacy teenage Jesus, after Sven was so heavily chided for including him in the England squad.

His two goals at Under-21 level are a cause for optimism. But what also concerns me is the succinct insight offered by West Ham alumnus Slaven Bilic. England, he correctly noted, are incapable of playing 3-5-2 – Ashley Cole and Gary Neville are full-backs and inevitably England will play with a five-man defence.

When hearing these comments I thought, 'Who knew this Slaven Bilic was concealing a neurological Catherine Wheel of tactical whizz-bangs?' Were it not for the appalling suit he wore, I'd be campaigning for him to become the next England manager.

Seems early, doesn't it, to be demanding that Steve McClaren be sacked, but that's what I am doing in this column. I think we have made a terrible mistake. I think McClaren became manager by default. It was only because of the FA's ghastly mishandling of the appointment of the next manager that it was not Phil Scolari presiding over the Croatia match. Can you honestly imagine England losing with that big, charismatic, swarthy sasquatch of a man in the dressing room? He would not permit defeat at the hands of a former Hammers upstart dressed in a suit that Burton would reject for being 'tawdry'.

One can scarcely condemn McClaren for accepting the job any more than one would damn a tinker for accepting the role of governor of the Bank of England. He's unlikely to say, 'You can poke your mint, I'm happy with my pots and pans.' Most football managers provoke incredible emotional reactions: 'arry 'arry Redknapp with his unreconstructed barra' boy charm, Sam Allardyce with his fierce northern passion, even Sven's professorial indifference provoked antipathy from fans. But McClaren is defined only by the fact that he is difficult to define. The unpopular meddling with his formation has proved to be desperately unwise and it does rile me somewhat that while Croatian fans can manage to formulate a perfect swastika in the stands, we can't even organise our own defence. Christ.

England don't play competitively for another five months, so there will be no real opportunity for this team to integrate. Perhaps by then Scolari, Martin O'Neill, or Allardyce and Alan Curbishley as some hilariously mismatched odd couple, could be in control of the national side. But if not, the panto season may continue long into the spring and our game against Israel in March will see the undignified spectacle of much-loved heroes playing like horses with two left feet and girls in roles traditionally occupied by men.

Football is dangerous so let's keep off the grass

21 October 2006

Ain't it intriguing to hear Chelsea stars dedicating their victory against Barcelona to Petr Cech. One don't imagine that kind of unity and sentimentality existing at the Billionaire Bridge. It ain't Jock Stein's Celtic, where the entire European Cup-winning team were born in one orphanage and played together for the honour of Glasgow. It's a cache of millionaires, cherry-picked from around the globe, and to hear 'em dedicating victories to each other is both heartening and a little suspicious.

It were a freakish affair, weren't it, Chelsea against Reading. To lose one goalkeeper to injury is unfortunate, to lose two looks reckless. I, for one, was overjoyed and over-excited, almost giggling up sick at the spectacle of John Terry slipping on the goalkeeper's jersey. Seeing Terry playing in goal gave me the same sense of excitement as when a dog gets into the playground at school.

'There's a dog in the playground, there's a dog in the playground!' Anarchy, no more lessons, abandon your posts, eat your crayons, the authority of the dinner lady is void. There shall be no work today as long as this hound is giddily scampering about the school yard. How can we learn anything other than all rules are meaningless?

Or when, as a child, a bird gets into your house and suddenly the place is alive with obstacles, the window panes are smeared with bird poo and the boundaries of life are suddenly shifting. Obviously, behind the thrill of seeing Terry in gloves is the seriousness of the injury. In a football match it's difficult to envisage a skull injury such as the one sustained by Cech. In fact, it's difficult to think of any jobs in which you might incur a skull injury, other than cage fighting or coconut juggling.

I don't play football myself, for the simple reason that it has always been a humiliating experience. I immediately lose all grace and posture when in pursuit of a ball. I adopt the air of a citizen of Pamplona fleeing a bull in that lethal festival they persist in having. The last time I played football was about five years ago, when I was still smoking quite a lot of grass. As is often the case in these situations, a friendly match between three or four of my mates attracted surrounding lads and ne'er-do-wells until eventually it became like an ancient game between rival villages, where a pig's bladder would be hoofed through rivers and across glens.

I remember that day – silly with weed, my astonishment at the physical aspect of the game, the horror at colliding with my brutish opponents. 'Man on! Man on!' someone would holler. 'Oh Christ,' I would think, booting the ball away, viewing my opponents as ball-seeking missiles. 'If I could just get rid of this ball then at least I'd be safe.'

I suppose only in that moment did I appreciate how dangerous the game can be. Recently, when Newcastle visited West Ham, their goalkeeper, Shay Given, sustained an injury after a difficult challenge and left Upton Park in an ambulance. The chant 'You're going home in an ambulance' now sounds less like a bellicose and implausible threat and more like a statement of fact. Fans might just as well sing 'What kind of fruit would you like at the hospital?'

I was trapped in the players' lounge while Given was carried out on a stretcher, and to see him prostrate and defeated momentarily peeled away the layers of loyalty and jocular aggression that surrounds football and made me think, 'Oh, bloody hell, poor Shay Given, he's hurt himself.' It's difficult to imagine footballers being so vulnerable or going through a crisis of confidence or a bad patch, when they seem so robust and confident and rich.

I am assured by various sources that Wayne Rooney's dip in form is due to a loss of confidence, and I know West Ham strikers like Bobby Zamora and Marlon Harewood are as marionettes to their own self-esteem. Zamora when confident, like Harewood, is worth a goal a game, but both suffer frequent lapses in form. They appear to have the mentality of musicians, or fine artists.

Only when footballers are injured do we recognise their fallibility, that they also exist outside an adult Disney World where they live on a diet of precious gems, enormous sponsorship deals and roasts. Only then do we see that they are human like us. One only has to look back on the last three major international tournaments and their trail of splintered metatarsals to see that these young men evoke religious devotion in us, with the *Sun* printing prayer mats to aid the speedy recovery of Beckham's foot. Before that there was Lineker's wrist, Greavsie's ankle and Lofthouse's lumbago.

Perhaps it's right that footballers live like gangster royalty – their career is a short one, their time in the limelight often cut off with little warning. Perhaps this week's events can remind us that these earthbound deities earn the devotion that we afford them.

The geezer-suffragette stands up to be counted

28 October 2006

Sometimes there can be a kind of euphoria to failure when, on occasion, a catastrophe can be so monumental, so spectacular, that it becomes almost blissful, like sleep deprivation or fasting. It's been so long now since West Ham have enjoyed a victory or even a draw that the failure itself becomes beautiful. When West Ham lost to Chesterfield, the sense of disappointment was so profound, lucid, livid and sharp that it almost plunged through the threshold of failure and attained a Zen-like state of detachment induced by disaster.

Why is it that happiness visits so seldom and stays so fleetingly, like an April butterfly alighting momentarily upon your finger, whereas tragedy lurks heavy in your guts like black and leaden porridge? Sullen. Eternally bleak.

You will be aware if you have followed this column that I offer tacit support to Andy Stephenson's Stand Up Sit

Down campaign, the aim of which is to enable West Ham fans to stand in designated areas of Upton Park. I told my friend Jack, a West Ham fan, about this protest and he chuckled at the nostalgic ideology of the campaign. 'Blimey, are they still protesting about that? They must be baffled by the modern game.'

'We want to stand up at matches', 'I want a rosette and one of them rattle things', ''Ere, why's the goalkeeper just picked up the ball?', 'They're using too many substitutes', 'What's happened to Lady Diana?'

However, I can understand these sentiments. When some men talk about their club the tone is familial. Andy's anger with Terence Brown, West Ham's chairman, is almost Oedipal. 'He's happy to spend our money. He never uses his own resources.' His sense of betrayal is intensely personal; the musty fug of mistrust is like the sort you'd project towards a sweaty-palmed uncle or an intoxicated mother.

I've gawn and got myself into a bit of a situation – members of the campaign plan to chain themselves to the main gates at West Ham before tomorrow's match against Blackburn. I was asked not to mention the specific nature of the protest, lest it be scuppered by my scribblings tipping awf the Peelers. I have now pledged that if this has any negative impact on the protest, I will, like a geezer-suffragette, chain myself to the railings in his stead in front of Sky's cameras. I already rue this oath. I reckon I've chained myself to a risky scenario. If the protesters are prevented from carrying out their direct action I'm going to find myself in an awful situation. Ironically, too, because, though I appreciate the desire of the campaigners to stand up during matches, I myself quite likes the occasional sit down.

I'm happy to stand up during some songs and of course when there's a goal but often I like to peruse the game all sedentary and snug, but what I must support is the right to stand. Again my mate Jack said he ain't worried about the fans standing up, he just wishes some of the players would stand up. 'Where's Nigel Reo-Coker?' he remarked. That's who he wants to stand up. What's happened to the player of last season?

It's easy to understand the nostalgia of some fans yearning for the game they grew up with, but has that gone forever? Can we ever return to the game we remember from our childhood? An ocean of men on Green Street, the numinous thrill of the emerging pitch as you rise from the tunnel into the stand? I sincerely bloody well hope so.

Recently I did an interview for West Ham's programme, which wasn't included because they belatedly found out that I am a recovering heroin addict. I was surprised by this censorship and narked off because one of the items was to name my all-time favourite West Ham team. Which, of course, with the exception of Bobby Moore, are the players I watched when I was growing up: Frank McAvennie, Mark Ward, Julian Dicks. Perhaps because now the only drug I am high on is nostalgia.

I hope tomorrow's game goes well, I hope the protest is triumphant, I hope I'm not forced to fling myself in front of the king's horses in an attempt to prove my allegiance not only to this beloved club but also to an idea that, like a butterfly of springtime joy, appears to be fluttering into an infinite winter.

Noel invokes the Christmas spirit of the terraces

4 November 2006

Twice this week I've found my identity submerged into the cloying comfort of the crowd: once at Upton Park for West Ham's victory against Blackburn, and once at the Koko venue in Camden to host a fundraising event headlined by Noel Gallagher.

The Blackburn win followed eight consecutive losses, West Ham's worst run of defeats for 74 years, but even before kick-off Alan Pardew's name was chanted with Gregorian devotion. This respect was hard won: Pards, as he's been awkwardly dubbed, was initially regarded with suspicion which, from an evolutionary perspective, is a sensible, if anachronistic, way to regard the alien. Now that the tumultuous rigours of birth have been endured a deeper affection has been engendered.

Pardew spoke of feeling 'choked and emotional' on hearing the fans' reception and I rather enjoyed the raucous tenderness that it suggested. Last season he guided West Ham to their first cup final in 20 years and achieved a very respectable position in the league, but the loyalty displayed last Sunday to me seemed to be more than the rational endorsement of previous success and the rejection of tabloid fervour. There was a delicious sentimentality that I've only ever encountered at matches and family Christmases, a kind of pie-eyed, beleaguered sense of unity, a rowdy, ill-considered, yet heartfelt love.

When Oasis swaggered into the public consciousness in the 90s it was as the voice of the simultaneous 'Lad' phenomenon and they were intrinsically associated with the terraces, booze and the 'white line'. Until Thursday night I'd never been at one of their gigs and had never encountered their fans en masse and, let me tell you, it was like no other musical event I've attended. I have become friends with Noel which is why he, along with Paul Weller, agreed to appear at the benefit for Focus12, the treatment centre for drug and alcohol addiction where I got clean, and of which I am now a patron.

I was under no illusions as to who the crowd had come to see on this occasion but thought the fifty quid ticket price and acoustic nature of the evening might mean a relatively passive audience. But when I came out to introduce the first act, The Holloways, the mosh-pit, which gurgled and churned like an intestine, was already chanting a name with the same bellicose commitment I'd encountered the previous Sunday at Upton Park and that name was not mine. I strained to ascertain the content of the mantra as one does when trying to divine the unfamiliar songs of away support – 'LI-AM, LI-AM'.

I glanced up to the balcony and there he was, to regard his elder brother's travails, Liam Gallagher. Even from that distance he certainly has presence. The crowd were friendly but vocal, passionate, and engaged all the qualities you expect at a match but not so much at a charity do. The Holloways were excellent but each time one of their songs finished the crowd would seize the opportunity to begin one of their own – exclusively odes to Manchester City's most prominent players (or perhaps playas, in a hip-hop way).

I realised quickly that my job as compere was to contain the maelstrom as much as possible, which wasn't easy (that's the thing about maelstroms, they're bloody difficult to contain) and limit the chanting to the bits between other bands – my bits, 'twere a selfless act. Dirty Pretty Things came on next and they too were remarkable and aided considerably, in the eyes of the pit, by the appearance of The Charlatans' charming Tim Burgess, who belongs to the era from which Oasis emerged.

I have never been more grateful to utter three words as the moment when I was finally able to say: 'Welcome, Noel Gallagher.' Once he began to perform I watched him and the crowd and pondered why he inspires such adulation. There were several points where the masses' rendition of his songs completely overwhelmed the sound from on stage, so it isn't an audio aesthetic with which they identify but something more profound.

A couple of things became apparent over the course of Noel's set: firstly, he is a song-writing genius with an almost paranormal ability to convert emotion into music; secondly, he has the power to capture and relate an unspoken longing, an atavistic yearning to be united, to be immersed into the social and untethered from the illusory constraints of the self. And where else can you get that? Upton Park. Sunday. West Ham v Arsenal.

Chants would be a fine thing if they weren't so rude

11 November 2006

I'm on tour at the moment and am frequently required to leave the cosy ant-hill fizz of London for gigs on weekend evenings. This often means departing matches at Upton Park before the final whistle. This was the case on Sunday when I left West Ham v Arsenal 15 minutes early, thus missing Marlon Harewood's last-minute goal and a spat between Alan Pardew and Arsene Wenger which, I later observed, resembled a quarrel between two wheezy Oxford dons.

My 'fighting talk' is pretty shoddy. Often I have resorted to pseudo-sexual taunts that are more macabre than threatening, for example once in a brawl at a comedy venue in Edinburgh I seethed at a doorman in what I perceived to be a menacing murmur worthy of Eastwood – 'Come on then, princess, do you wanna dance round my garden?' I only know this because an eyewitness informed me retrospectively, as my own memory was affected by the tornadoes of blows that immediately followed that camp fatwa.

Pardew, while gentle and English, seems to me capable of 'rumble rhetoric', but a slur from Wenger, however aggressive, must feel like being slandered by Molière. The real hostility in that game was between the West Ham fans and Robin van Persie, an antagonistic presence who for the better part of the game oscillated between jaunty runs and futile diving.

Van Persie was the recipient of some viciously sharp chants too cruel to print, but in the moment I naturally joined the chorus, which was awkward really because I sit next to a 15-year-old girl and my companion that day was also female. So when a chant commenced libellously damning Van Persie as the worst kind of criminal, or even a lighter number started up extolling the virtues of East London as a haven for 'tits, fanny and West Ham', I fell quiet and eyed my female sentries apologetically.

The apex of the antagonistic relationship between Van Persie and the crowd came when he was struck by a projectile penny and tumbled earthward like the Tower of Babel. Of course, I don't condone this behaviour, if for no other reason than I'd begrudge him the wage increase, but it didn't 'alf seem to hurt him – the song 'Pennies From Heaven' must to him seem like a dystopian nightmare.

The most ubiquitous of all chants would have to be 'The referee's a wanker' sung in a plethora of dialects, from

Portsmouth to Newcastle. For all I know, there may be a version in Esperanto. In the Arsenal game it was deemed apposite and increasingly it seems that it's an anthem for our times.

Graham Poll appears to be working tirelessly to make it his personal jingle in the sitcom that is his career, issuing cards with the indiscriminate desperation of an isolated neighbour at Christmas. Match officials are seldom regarded as benevolent but I've heard men give vent to such splenetic antipathy as to query where this black-rage came from.

At a cup match last season I was with my mate Ade who yells incessantly, but mostly in good humour. He's in a chair so we are sat in the disabled section. Adjacent was a man with his quadraplegic son – both were pleasant and we chatted, but after kick-off he greeted each blast of the whistle with such unfettered rage that I felt unnerved listening to his hotly spluttered laments. They were consistent in that all were fierce invective against the unjust authority of the ref. 'Why, REF!?'

I sensed this fury at injudicious authority was ultimately intended for an indifferent God that had delivered him on these difficult days a rage against the games he'll never see his son play.

When Teddy Sheringham scored against Blackburn the game before Arsenal, the roar was of relief, a recognition that things can go right. My own cascading joy was drawn from a place not specific to football but a release from all the doubt I've ever felt. And while the referee might be a wanker he's not as bad as my old headmaster or cold, cold circumstance.

Celestial troubadour or gay disco icon? You decide

18 November 2006

Regular readers of this column will be aware that I'm fascinated to the point of fetish with football chants. I'm a West Ham supporter and the Hammers have as their anthem what I believe to be the greatest terrace hit: 'Bubbles'.

It encapsulates perfectly the nature of transience, the impossibility of true success, and if adapted can be used to taunt both Arsenal and Tottenham. Instead of 'fortune always hiding, I've looked everywhere' you can sing: 'Arsenal always hiding, Tottenham running scared. I'm forever blowing bubbles, blowing bubbles in the air.'

But at the last home match Arsenal fans barracked the Claret and Blue army with the line 'you've only got one song' – offensive and untrue. The repertoire is strong. 'Stick Your Blue Flag Up Your Arse' is a considered, succinct attack on Chelsea. 'West Ham Till I Die' is sung to the tune of 'H-A-P-P-Y', and 'Over Land and Sea' is sung to the tune of 'Land of Hope and Glory'. Occasionally a new number will emerge – 'Zamora' to the tune of 'Volare' – but I believe that was plagiarised from Arsenal and it was originally Vieira.

Even had I not been inspired by this recent taunt from the McGunners (see the McGunners live from the Emirates Stadium) I've been long troubled by the lack of original terrace material. There's a gentleman called Pete Boyle at Manchester United who constantly replenishes the Stretford End with chants. I recently perused some of his catalogue, a particular favourite being an ode to Roy Keane, to the tune of 'My Old Man's a Dustman', although it does include a confusing line about Roy Keane wearing a magic hat, which to my mind he does not and never has.

I mentioned before that I would never have the confidence to be the first to stand up and commence a terrace chant. I view the men that have the courage to do this as heroes fallen from the stars, celestial troubadours descended from the heavens to deliver us these melodies. But in the privacy of my boudoir I have happened upon what I believe could be a stadium chart-topper. Even as I write this tentatively – my fingers all aquiver, such is the trepidation that I feel about sharing this secret – it seems to me that the song 'Uptown Girl' by Billy Joel might easily become a beloved of West Ham fans if, instead of 'Uptown Girl, she's been living in her uptown world', came the cry 'Upton Park, we're the Hammers, we're from Upton Park'.

Now, this I know ain't much but, after all, do not mighty horse chestnut trees grow from tiny acorns? I would like to hereby start a campaign to complete this song. I did toy with the idea of (and remember Billy Joel's rhythm as you read this) 'Upton Park, we're the Hammers, we're from Upton Park. We're just a bunch of East End boys . . .'

But when I suggested this to a friend and fellow West Ham fan he said it sounded less like a football chant and more like a Village People cover of a much loved song. That might make me a gay disco icon but would be unlikely to win me any friends in the Premiership. Therefore from this moment forth I would like to commence a campaign for us all to rejuvenate the depleted stocks of football terrace chants. Please send me your ideas, not only to complete the brilliant kernel that I've begun but also fresh ideas of your own.

Perhaps before the end of the season the football grounds of the United Kingdom will ring out with brilliant, novel and original songs, and obviously I need input, for if it were left up to me there would be naught but frilly ballads and nancy-boy nursery rhymes. I plan to promote this idea further on my Radio 2 show which starts tonight at 9 o'clock and it is my intention that by West Ham's home game against Sheffield United the lyrics to Upton Park will be complete and I will stand, hand on hips, at the front of the North Bank singing it, if necessary, in a claret and blue leotard hurling a majorette baton skyward.

Magnusson's spark will pull Upton Park from the dark

25 November 2006

I am a supporter of West Ham United and the takeover of the club by the Icelandic millionaire Eggert Magnusson heralds a new golden age for the Hammers. Like a yin yang conundrum played out in human flesh, Kia Joorabchian and Magnusson fought for the soul of West Ham United, and most supporters I talked to seem to think that the best man won.

My only concern is that Magnusson is head of the Icelandic FA, and if people that head the Icelandic FA are anything like the English FA, Magnusson may well be a shambolic indecisive atavistic loon ransacking the past for pipe dreams and schemes. If, however, the Icelandic FA are not like the English FA, he might be a thoroughly good chap. It's a positive thing for example that he's a football fan but not so positive that his allegiance previously was to Tottenham Hotspur, a club for whom the Claret and Blue army lack affection.

I worry because West Ham is such a familiar club. I became friendly with one of the security staff at the ground and he told me that, having worked there for 18 years, he was still the newest member of the security team. It's that kind of longevity that West Ham offers to their backroom staff although, on the pitch, Carlos Tevez and Javier Mascherano look set to leave in the near future.

Magnusson has also backed Alan Pardew, which is a positive thing. The manager is so beloved of West Ham fans that he was granted an incredibly extended grace period through the recent spell of eight consecutive defeats. This was not just because of last season's fantastic form and Cup final appearance but a sense of guilt that early in his reign he was treated with suspicion and contempt and that guilt to some degree lingers on, and affords him latterly more sympathy.

I hope that Magnusson and Pardew can together forge a new era at West Ham. The new chairman has spoken of aiming for a Champions League place. While it might be fanciful to talk of a Champions League position for the Hammers, why don't we indulge that fantasy for a moment? While we're at it, let's also imagine that, perhaps next season during a Champions League qualifying match, Upton Park might explode in unison into a glorious chorus of Billy Joel's 'Uptown Girl'. Or rather the Russell Brand version, 'Upton Park', which I am currently working on both in this column and on my Radio 2 show.

Please email me your alternative lyrics not only to this song but also to other songs to create more invigorating and enlivening chants to provide a brighter future for West Ham and any club you choose.

So far the Billy Joel 'Uptown Girl' Russell Brand version goes: 'Upton Park, we're the Hammers, we're from Upton Park'. Having received endorsements in print we are going with the line, 'We're just a bunch of East End boys, now we're going to make some effing noise, some effing noise.' Imagine that to the tune of 'Uptown Girl', I think you'll see it works. Within one short year we will be singing that song at Camp Nou. I'll be at the front with pompoms and a bra, wiggling my sweet little tush as the travelling pride of West Ham fans do harmonies in the 'Whoa ooooooooo' bit.

Now let's get on with our glorious Icelandic future, by which I mean clean, rich and plentiful, not the perpetual darkness of a never-ending night.

How to ruck in Green Street, courtesy of Enid Blyton

2 December 2006

Having recently, unthinkingly, embarked on a campaign to rejuvenate terraces with new and frankly camp chants, I have been astonished by the response I have provoked.

I'm aware that's a media cliché – whenever *Blue Peter* had an appeal they erupted into unlikely hyperbole, announcing that the weight of pledges had induced an eternal springtime in the Percy Thrower garden. 'Ne'er more shall it know winter and the tortoise won't be boxward jammed.' That said, I've had loads of emails suggesting fantastic songs and lyrics – too many to list here. Suffice to say there's a chant based on 'Sheila Take A Bow', a Spurs ballad derived from 'Come On Eileen' and a Wolverhampton shanty inspired by 'Subterranean Homesick Blues'. All ingenuity sparked by my 'umble adaptation of 'Uptown Girl'.

I inadvertently reprised this chant on my Channel 4 show at the behest of Arsenal fan Matt Lucas, incurring a £5,000 fine from the publishers, which seems a tad mean. In the unlikely event Billy Joel ever unwittingly uses the words 'ballbags' or 'citing' I shall not spare the rod.

I hope the attention is merited and not the sympathetic niceties afforded to the disadvantaged, like an unloved child packed off to EuroDisney in an ill-fitting cap. Jeremy Nicholas, the announcer at Upton Park, in an act of kindness that makes Florence Nightingale seem a vindictive misanthrope, played 'Uptown Girl' at half-time during West Ham's win against Sheffield United, attempting to induce the crowd to sing my effete anthem.

I feel now rather bashful about the campaign, due in no small part to a recent viewing of the film *Green Street*, in which a hobbit becomes a 'soccer hooligan'. I happen to know a good many talented people were involved, but the end result is rather confusing. It is an attempt to romanticise the fraternity between members of football firms, in this case the fictional Green Street Elite or GSE – which made me wonder why they couldn't just say ICF. Perhaps it was for legal reasons, or perhaps for fear of a thrashing, in which case I should shut up. But they made hooliganism look like a quarrel between two gangs from Enid Blyton. Also, the lead character's accent gives Dick Van Dyke's 'Mowry Purpins' turn an air of chilling, Loach-like authenticity.

There are several scenes where genuine chants are used and I'll wager they used real fans as extras. These scenes at least seemed honest, particularly compared with the clockwork jocundity of the chatter between the leads, but I felt that clandestine culture ought not to be plundered for base entertainment and it made me think that perhaps I am guilty, in my attempt to turn the chicken run into a chorus line of Billy Joel sissies, of a similar offence.

While I am a lifelong Hammers fan, begat by a Hammers fan – my dad's mum's Orient – I could never be described as hardcore. Look at my hairdo, for God's sake. So is it right to continue to attempt to infiltrate the terraces with jaunty ditties, or am I like a deluded missionary barging into an aboriginal village and dishing out boob-inspector caps and sherbet dips?

Were the chant to be embraced, it might induce the lachrymose panic I feel on birthdays, Christmas parties or any occasion where happiness is prescribed. I would, I fear, become overwhelmed by the disproportionate gratitude that blights the Elephant Man – 'Oh you're so kind, you sang "Upton Park" to the tune of "Uptown Girl"!' What perturbs me is my suspicion that the root of Project Joel is my yearning to be accepted by men like my father and stepdad – physical, footballing men comfortable in the rowdy company of fellas – and yet my preposterous method for that undertaking is to make the Boleyn Ground throb with camp caterwauling.

Daft really. Perhaps I ought just to enjoy the crowd, an enthralled tourist, ever doubting my credentials. As I mentioned before, I sit next to a 15-year-old girl in the Doc Martens Stand. I'm not sandwiched between the

Krays and Ray Winstone. When I stop thinking and watch the football and chant, I'm taken out of myself, the individual submerged into the whole and that, I suspect, is football's primal force, this mystical ability to unite. I suppose this week I'll ponder whether this utopia needs to be garnished with chintzy songs. Let me know your views – and keep sending your chants.

Utopia, unity and Hammers' homoerotic song

9 December 2006

I was unable to attend West Ham's home game against Wigan and so in a feat of altruism that equals anything you're likely to read about in the New Testament I gave my season tickets to my assistant, Helen, and her girlfriend. Yes, that's right, my assistant Helen is a lesbian, and I never seek to make capital out of this fact ('Ah, my friend Helen is a lesbian thus I understand the works of Jeanette Winterson almost innately'). Once more I refer to the earlier comment about my biblical altruism: I never use my knowledge of her lifestyle choices to taunt or berate her.

As well as being gay she is also American and she and her girlfriend, Shazzy, took the place of me and my plus one for the game. I was intrigued to hear her interpretation of the match. Helen grew up in Los Angeles and is more accustomed to attending Lakers basketball games than what she still insists on terming 'soccer matches'. 'Don't say that near the Chicken Run,' I nervously intoned.

Her match report was intriguing to listen to. She was enthralled by the game and enormously enjoyed the thrill of a live sporting event but was struck by the stark contrast between American and English sport. She said, and I quote: 'At a Lakers game you could be inches from Jack Nicholson or Leonardo DiCaprio.'

Well that's unlikely at Upton Park. You might bump into Noel Edmonds or Ray Winstone and, dare I say it, myself, but watching me cheering Matty Etherington in my shrill falsetto must come a poor second to watching Tobey Maguire slapping Magic Johnson on the back.

I mentioned, in passing, in my last article that I have a perpetual sense of alienation which accompanies me through life, and occasionally it stirs during West Ham home matches. The supportive emails that I have received astonished me, one in particular from a young woman, also a Hammers fan, who describes herself as not being a bloke-ish bird but as dressing 'all feminine'. She writes delicately and with the celestial majesty of Blake describing angels in Peckham Rye when explaining her experiences behind the goal on the North Bank, causing me to fall in love with the abstract idea of this woman.

I also received further brilliant suggestions for chants, one person noting I oughtn't berate myself for the suggestion of Billy Joel's 'Uptown Girl' as a potential anthem as West Ham's signature tune 'Bubbles' does include the pseudo homoerotic line 'I'm forever blowing bubbles' first used in reference to a West Ham player in the 1920s with the nickname Bubbles. If anyone has any more information on this I'd be intrigued to hear it.

This email and Helen's experience at Upton Park made me consider the nature of inclusion and exclusivity at football matches. I was already pondering this theme when I got into my car this morning and the driver, Mathew, who arrived from Trinidad in the 1960s, told me he supported West Ham. Despite living in north London ever since his arrival, he was a Hammer because of West Ham's style, and the finesse and the grace of the men who played football. He said he stopped attending matches in the early 80s because of the violence and racism but he still spoke of a deep love for West Ham, becoming almost misty eyed at the mention of Billy Bonds. He almost recited the 'West Ham till I die' mantra. 'I love West Ham, I'll always love West Ham,' he said. Mathew was a person I instantly liked.

George Orwell, in his book *Homage to Catalonia*, in which he relates his experiences fighting against Franco in the Spanish civil war, speaks about meeting another recruit for POUM on the day he enlisted whom he instantly liked. This instant human connection can sometimes feel almost divine between two people and I felt it on meeting Mathew, a sense of immediate comfort.

When feeling that sense of inclusion, that sense of shared humanity in the enhanced context of a crowd of 34,000 as one sometimes does at football matches, it is a sensation approaching the utopian. And I suppose that's what keeps us all attending football matches whether you feel like you belong there or not. I hope that Helen, my American lesbian assistant (did I mention that?), will continue to attend West Ham matches, I hope Mathew will return to the terraces and I hope that I, too, will be able to attend football matches as I largely do feeling united and embraced – united by something bigger than us, bigger than our differences, bigger even than West Ham United.

Pardew is scrambled and Curbishley is poached – another week in the life of West Ham's golden Egg

16 December 2006

Our capacity to be shocked by the inevitable is seemingly boundless. Each celebrity death that you read about in the news is greeted with tidal waves of astonished grief. Extra-marital affairs evoke confusion and the sacking of football managers still raises bafflement when really it oughtn't even raise an eyebrow. It is as inevitable as the relentless march of time, the erosion of the ozone layer, the depletion of North Sea fish stock and festive tabloid stories bemoaning the ill-deserved luxury of prison Christmas dinners.

The mood among my friends who are West Ham followers is one of glum acceptance. I was labelled a turncoat earlier in the season when after eight successive defeats I, prophetically now I see, suggested that Alan Curbishley might be a good replacement for Alan Pardew. What better time for West Ham to receive a saviour than Christmas. Although Curbishley could be regarded as a rather humdrum

Messiah, I feel confident and excited by the appointment. One of my friends said it's replacing like for like and certainly it's true that both men have the faint whiff of a benevolent stepfather about them. For me Curbishley's time at Charlton and his constant resistance to the tide of relegation that must have yearned to consume them makes his a favourable appointment.

One feels that Curbishley will not favour the kind of cheque-book management that would be ill-fitting for a club such as the Hammers. Even if Eggert Magnusson does give him a treasure chest, his thrifty years at The Valley will put him in good stead – he's unlikely to scuttle over to the Bridge in an attempt to seduce Shaun Wright-Phillips. Unlike Glenn Roeder, a manager who I imagine is simply sitting with a pile of cash by his left hand and a list of available players by his right, giddily cross referencing with a pin.

Eggert Magnusson is a man whose name is a gift to Premiership football; not since Arsene Wenger has a name been more pertinent. Magnusson has the word 'egg' in his name, is bald and his head looks a bit like an egg, easily affording him the nickname 'The Egg'. It has already taken off among my friends, not a long mental journey but none the less satisfying to say.

It was interesting how quickly his pledge of support led to a sacking. I wonder what he meant when he said 'Yes, Alan Pardew is a part of our long-term plans for this club.' Did he mean that in the infinite universe a second could be an eternity and therefore a couple of weeks are equivalent to thousands of lifetimes?

I'm curious about when the decision was made. I think it was caused by the defeats by Everton and Wigan in quick succession in conjunction with the shoddy performances of most of the players and the reported 'loss of the dressing room'. There's a phrase you never used to hear. I don't like to think of them sat in a dressing room with mirrors framed with lights applying greasepaint and not saying 'Macbeth'. It all sounds a bit fruity.

These things combined are a force difficult to define. My mate told me that in the olden days tribal kings were exalted throughout their lives. They were shrouded in glory, serviced by virgins, they gorged on quail eggs and other delicacies, but all this luxury was merely a prelude to the moment when they were sacrificed to a merciless god. Being a football manager is rather like that. So let's enjoy this period where Curbishley is carried in a sedan down Green Street, spoken of as a potential saviour. Kept out of the side by Trevor Brooking during his career at the Boleyn now he may join the pantheon of West Ham managerial greats, alongside John Lyall, Ron Greenwood and Harry Redknapp. A firmament of cockney legends.

Sup deeply dear Alan, enjoy this feted period, for surely soon enough the day will come when the virgins and quail eggs will all be spent and in their stead will be a grim dagger, concealed behind the bonce of a benevolent egg man.

Magic win but Curbs to our enthusiasm remain

23 December 2006

It were a glorious victory against Manchester United last Sunday. Alan Curbishley on his debut created utopia. One banner hung limply, declaring loyalty to Alan Pardew, scarcely visible in the rafters. A slogan scrawled upon a bedsheet will be Pardew's eulogy, then, but his legacy is a core of young players, many of whom were snatched from obscurity by his keen eye and trained to Premiership standards by his methods. But now is the era of Curbishley. How apposite that it should commence with a goal from Nigel Reo-Coker, a player who has been absent from the team, if not physically then very much spiritually and mentally. He has been but a shadow cast by the vapour of the player he was last season.

It was my favourite game this season. There was an incredible spirit of unity and after Reo-Coker's goal I was embraced by people I don't yet know. Hugs were fired at me from all directions and if churches could conjure such a sense of unity they would be full throughout the yuletide season.

I was surprised to read in Olas (Over Land And Sea), West Ham's brilliantly written fanzine, of the incredible depth of loyalty towards Pardew. Even though fans are happy about Curbishley's arrival there is a great deal of regret about Pardew's departure. I think what upsets people is the suggestion that his sacking might signify a new commercial era which the club has done well thus far to stave off. There aren't that many clubs like West Ham in Premiership football now – perhaps Portsmouth, perhaps Newcastle – where there is a sense that the club is, to a degree, owned by the fans. The nature of commercial enterprise is necessarily the death of this social ideal and now talk again abounds of the club moving to a new ground in Stratford after the Olympics and a rash of foreign imports.

I'm not against progress – I'd like to see West Ham competing for major honours. There is nothing quite like seeing them defeating United or Arsenal. How can any club beat those teams and still feel the icy hand of relegation resting upon their shoulder? But I hope they don't detach themselves from the ethos that makes them special.

My other cause for concern is the news that Reo-Coker has received racist death threats. I suppose if you receive death threats the ideology behind them is insignificant. A racist death threat, a sexist death threat, a homophobic death threat – I imagine that the death-threat aspect is what worries you most. The prejudice, I suppose, is just further evidence of antipathy. The reason for this hate mail is presumed to be that Reo-Coker has been implicated in the Pardew sacking saga. But who sends hate mail? What kind of way is that to communicate? I feel nervous sending text messages to my friends. I don't know how people get themselves in the frame of mind to send racist hate mail.

Reo-Coker is but a human being. I once met him at a party and was astonished that this hero captain of my club was in fact barely a man. Very much a teenager. Just out of short trousers – still wears 'em at weekends. So to make him the target of such acrimony is not befitting. I suppose it just demonstrates how important football is to some people and how insignificant morality and spiritual truth.

Although the victory over United can be viewed as a triumph, the highlight had to be when, after the game as the once mighty crowd dwindled into a trickle, I was spotted by two fans. As they passed me one yawped, in a tone that was both jocular and mocking: 'Upton Park, we're the Hammers, we're from Upton Park.' Then his mate chimed in, holding his lapels in a musical style and affecting a camp jiggle. 'We're just a bunch of East End boys.' They then chuckled by.

This to me was a proud moment. To hear my chant, if not sung en masse upon the terrace, I have achieved some level of penetration. This has reignited my enthusiasm for the campaign and I shall redouble my efforts. If anything, I need to aim higher. Perhaps for the next home game, against Portsmouth, instead of singing 'Upton Park' to the tune of Billy Joel's 'Uptown Girl' I can inspire the Chicken Run to sing 'Y.M.C.A.' with accompanying camp actions. With Curbishley in charge, the sky's the limit.

Death is beautiful but Wright-Phillips means life

6 January 2007

I get a kind of giddy adolescent thrill during periods of intense transfer activity, like a pre-prom frisson in an American teen romcom. 'Ooh, did Chad invite you to the prom?' 'Are you wearing that peach frock?' 'Did you hear Luis Boa Morte has signed for West Ham?' 'Tis a time of transition and hope renewed.

Though in the case of Boa Morte, the signs are mixed: his name literally translates into 'Luis Beautiful Death' – which is a bit heavy. Good portent for the oncoming relegation struggle, d'ya think? Beautiful Death? Like a swan in a glittery waistcoat speared on a shard of black ice. A sentimental man could be forgiven for collapsing into a nostalgic reverie, lamenting 'Clever' Trevor Brooking's all too brief tenure when the Irons were relegated with more points than any Premiership club in history.

It is a time of Jacobean twists at Upton Park, under the stewardship of the Icelandic Egg-man (Goo goo g'joob).

Curbs from a post-Charlton wilderness, Pards to Charlton, ousted but with dignity intact and a misty veil of noble grief settling round East London's wounded streets. Ah, how the euphoria of the debut victory against United were swiftly replaced with plunging woe after the 6-0 slaughter at the hands of Championship foes Reading. Oh undue haste, oh bitter taste at glorious waste of mercurial fortune.

Yossi Benayoun reportedly claimed that West Ham played like 'a bunch of drunks'. I think any self-respecting drunk would rather choke on his vomit than endure such humiliation. Also, drunks can be quite single-minded in the pursuit of a goal. Perhaps the team ought to consider downing a tactical bottle of Thunderbird before away fixtures in future – at least, were they to score, the post-goal celebrations would be fun as the sublimated homoeroticism bloomed into full penetration, which would be good for bonding and help amend the antiquated attitude that exists towards homosexuality in football.

Having said that, Matt Lucas said he was greeted with earnest salutations at the Emirates Stadium, home of the McGunners, after his civil partnership with his partner Kevin. 'Well done on the wedding, mate' is a step in the right direction when you consider the trials of Justin Fashanu.

So the transfer patio door remains wide open and who would not dare to dream what else might come dancing through? Perhaps by the time you read this Javier Mascherano will be at Anfield and Shaun Wright-Phillips at West Ham at a considerable loss to Chelsea, which would make it doubly sweet. So here's a bit of inappropriate gossip for ya.

I've just come back from my holiday in Mauritius – jolly nice it was too – where also guesting at the humble shack where I resided was everybody's favourite oligarch, Roman Abramovich, which neatly quashed any doubts I had about the quality of the hotel. 'Ah,' I thought (which is a silly thing to think, really), 'there's one of earth's wealthiest men. This place must be all right.' One can scarcely imagine Roman tolerating Pontins and gamely participating in the coercive glee of that idiot crocodile that blighted my childhood summers.

I was drawn to Roman – he does rather exude power and on New Year's Eve, when the hotel held a buffet (a posh one with ice sculptures, not paper plates with pictures of balloons on them), I kept staring at him like an anxious spinster. When our eyes met, on three occasions, I tried to frame my features into an expression which, if verbalised, would say: 'Oh, hello mate, I'm off the telly, you needn't feel threatened or irritated – let's have a chin wag. After all, it's Christmas.' He responded with an expression that I interpreted as: 'You are an insignificant scuttle-bug and I could crush you with an eyelash.'

I told someone of this and they said, 'He's shy.' Perhaps that's true. Perhaps his shyness comes across as terrifying, awesome power. But I seem to recall The Smiths saying 'shyness is nice' not 'shyness is a cold stare that rips through your tender soul and leaves you gasping on a veranda wearing a paper hat that now cruelly mocks you, its joyless wearer, for your face is etched in fear and you are the king of naught but shame'. That's not 'nice'. I'm not judging him, though, let me get that in print. I'm sure he's lovely. I get nervous enough visiting the Bridge. Perhaps next time I go the Hammers will be in possession of Wright-Phillips and we'll avoid beautiful death and enjoy a humdrum victory.

Like an old dog looking for a quiet place to die

13 January 2007

When I think of Soccerball in connection with the United States, I recall depictions of hooligans in *The Simpsons*, children and women playing a neutered, *Escape to Victory* version of the game (not like Arsenal Ladies who seem robust – I'm not being sexist; racist possibly but not sexist) and Alexei Lalas's beard (I think in this image he's leaping to score a header at some point during Italia 90).

And it is to this land of preposterous imagery and inherent indifference to our game that David Beckham will run out his last few seasons of dead-ball excellence and razor endorsements. There was talk of him coming to West Ham or possibly Newcastle or Bolton, which I suppose would have seemed like a mistake, as if he were returning chastised, sans accomplishments, to be frustrated on some unloved, unlovely wing glancing to the centre of the action where he'd always been culturally and always yearned to be tactically.

I remember the night before our dog died she wouldn't sit with us, preferring instead to linger behind the sofa with the instinctive knowledge of her demise, and while California is more glamorous than the back of a settee in Essex I think that Beckham is too proud to let us witness his decline. Also I understand he's being quite well paid. Doubtless it appeals that he may be the footballing missionary who finally succeeds where Pele, Franz Beckenbauer and George Best failed and convinces America to enjoy a globally relevant activity other than bombing.

For what it's worth I like him. I like his vanity, his style, class and temperament. I didn't get swept up in the effigy burning (not that it was a national pursuit, my mum didn't either), I liked it that he wore a sarong and clearly tended to his hair at half-time during World Cup matches. As a footballer he's provided us with incredible moments, perhaps most notably the free kick he scored against Greece that granted qualification that would have otherwise been denied, and also awoke me from a heroin-induced stupor and gave me sufficient vim to order a pizza and make it through a difficult weekend.

There must be countless stories of acts of inadvertent kindness enacted by Beckham. Culturally only Diana has occupied the position of maligned and worshipped saint, adored for sartorial elegance, presumed dumb, ubiquitous yet endlessly fascinating. Perhaps because his communication skills aren't as sharp as his football skills he becomes enigmatic and endlessly intriguing. What is he thinking? What's he like in bed? Does he love his missus?

I've just begun working out with a personal trainer, an ex-footballer communicative only on the subject of fitness. This makes him a canvas on to which I project all manner of quirky fantasies, not sexual, just idle musings of how he'd be in a fight or a deerstalker. Dear David bears the burden of a nation's reflections.

He's not a tragic character, is he? Like Di? I hope not. I imagine all will be well for him in LA. They'll become chums with Snoop Dogg and continue their peculiar friendship with Tom and Katie Cruise. Perhaps they'll become Scientologists – that'd be nice (my American pc knows how to spell 'Scientologist' but not 'footballing' – that's worrying).

I hope his ambitions are the achievement of personal happiness, as opposed to some doomed crusade to make Americans like football. In my lifetime they've hosted one World Cup and reached the quarter-final of another and seem to delight in ignoring it. Whether they continue to be ignorant of the magic of the game he has so beautifully served is anybody's guess, but they'll struggle to ignore Beckham.

From Poll to poll: my week of controversy

20 January 2007

Given the fact that for six days a week I work for a *Big Brother* spin-off show it is rather difficult to draw my focus from the international hoopla that's been created by events inside the house. Last Saturday I watched West Ham draw with Fulham. It were a nerve-jangling affair and where Graham Poll produced five minutes of added injury-time from is a mystery to me. Perhaps it was from the same orifice from whence he plucked the third yellow card he dealt in the World Cup.

Neither side seemed content with Poll's adjudication that day. The Fulham fans thought he was awful as well. The West Ham fans stayed a further five minutes in addition to the five mystery minutes that he added on to chorus him down the tunnel with jaunty ballads of hate. I didn't imagine for a moment the words 'Graham Poll' and 'wanker' could be arranged in such vast and varying configurations.

West Ham have now entered into the transfer market, purchasing Calum Davenport, and at the time of writing it looks like Lucas Neill may join in addition to Luis Boa Morte and Nigel Quashie, both of whom played well on Saturday, not to the high standard achieved by Nigel Reo-Coker and the fantastic Yossi Benayoun but good performances from new players none the less. Eggert Magnusson is not shy in spending his Icelandic biscuit tokens, and it's a good thing because one cannot ignore West Ham's defence when allocating blame for Saturday's draw even though Poll contributed a goal of blunders to Fulham's final tally.

Whilst I've continued to follow Premiership football closely, my head has been swimming in controversy because of events in *Big Brother*. Of course racism is deplorable and bullying detestable – I wouldn't seek to query that. What I'm finding enormously difficult, as someone who has met Jade Goody on several occasions and can attest to the fact that she's a decent girl who's had a remarkably difficult life, is the notion that she's a bad person.

I don't know Danielle Lloyd or Jo from S Club 7 but I imagine they too in isolation are decent people. What irks me as much as the persecution of the elegant and beautiful Shilpa Shetty is the national wrath directed at these three women who are really expressing views and attitudes endemic in the culture from which they came. Of course football and racism went hand in hand for many years. There are many more black and Asian supporters at West Ham now than when I came as a child in the early 80s. But I suppose what is difficult about the *Big*

Brother fiasco and surrounding hullabaloo is that it's an indication of unaddressed racism throughout our culture. And to tell you the truth it's a right pain in the ass.

I suppose it will be a slow and thorough process that brings about a huge social change required to address these issues. Currently it's not so prevalent in football but it was not that long ago that John Barnes and Tony Daley were pelted with bananas whenever they played away.

Now the problem seems to have been quelled but perhaps if we were to watch the actions and conversations of football fans for 24 hours a day or indeed football players we would uncover things that were unpalatable – my only hope is that we can find in ourselves the compassion that we demand of those three housemates when it comes to judging them.

I am happy to do a sex dance for Luis Boa Morte

27 January 2007

Faith is a powerful tool in navigating us through life on our silly journey to inevitable death. Sometimes I believe in things simply because not to believe in them would make my life unbearable. I like to think that my cat, Morrissey, loves me and that his affection is not simply a tool to avoid starvation.

Apparently new-born infants affect the facial formation of a smile long before they understand what they're conveying just so they look sweet and their parents don't dash their brains out on the wall of the cave (this technique was pioneered by caveman babies when infanticide was more common).

If the sweet gurgling grin of a tot is up for question and even the loyalty of my cat, how can I so blindly believe that Lucas Neill has joined West Ham for the honour of wearing the claret and blue shirt and not for the reported sixty grand a week he's being paid (I think that's what

Paul Scholes gets that puts things in too much perspective)? When it's suggested, as it often has been over the past few weeks that Neill snubbed Rafa Benitez and the Kop because he fancied the cockney dollar I bristle.

Surely it's better to play your football in East London under intense pressure to avoid relegation than to faff around on Merseyside perpetually under-achieving (penalty shoot-outs aside) trying to recreate the boot room glory days. It is. It's much better and that's why dear sweet, noble Lucas has come to Upton Park. He likes a challenge and, as he said himself, Curbishley has a shopping list that made his goolies fizz.

I hope it's a sensible investment – admittedly West Ham's chief problems, atrocious refereeing aside, appear to be defensive and one queries how much impact even the most versatile and influential full-back can have. The Hammers legend Julian Dicks played on the opposite flank to Neill and were capable of dragging the team along with pure aggression and I suppose Gary Neville is a potent force at United but is he as important as Scholes?

The simple fact is West Ham need players and are in no position to quibble over trifling matters such as wages. If Nigel Quashie demands his income be supplemented by spending half-time with The Hammerettes (the team's cheerleaders) I think it ought be granted. In fact, if it can guarantee us Premiership survival, I myself am happy to troop out in the interval with the mascots – the hammer, the bear and the inexplicable dog in a blue nurse's uniform – and perform a humiliating sex dance for Luis Boa Morte, such is my desire to see those boys happy.

A friend described West Ham as a rubbish Chelsea, with our tin-pot, bickie rich, Kojak oligarch and unglamorous signings. But it appears the dominion of the blue flag may be on the wane. Jose Mourinho is, it seems, a rather quixotic character, a tactical troubadour only content to remain at a club for a couple of seasons before moving on. In fact he's like the littlest hobo – he does terrific work then clears off leaving John Terry with a frog in his throat cos' 'there's a voice that keeps on calling him'.

Poor JT all injured and heartbroken, can the dream really be over already? The blue flag yanked down from its pole to dry Drogba's tears? 'Twere always likely that it would end in ignominy – you can't purchase tradition and pedigree. One assumes the glory days will return to Anfield, it's in their blood, but Chelsea were always gonna crumble, slung together, a papier mache empire made from pound notes and the tears of Stanley Matthews weeping for football's egalitarian dream. The Irons will stay up, powered by Neill's unequivocal loyalty but the Blue Tower shall fall.

Relegation rants are West Ham's songs of experience

3 February 2007

Any follower of a club perpetually threatened by relegation will recognise a chilling moment that occurs as the season reaches its close, a stark moment of clarity, too visually shrill to acknowledge but unignorable in its primary coloured boldness. As cruel as the blossoming beauty of an adolescent daughter to the eye of her menopausal mother – indecent, vicious nature with her calamitous, indifferent tricks.

The moment of which I speak but fear almost too greatly to name is one I myself endured this Tuesday night watching West Ham against Liverpool. After Liverpool's second goal and the lacklustre response of the crestfallen Hammers, the dreaded thought, clammy and uninvited, slithered through my fragile mind like the gleeful boot of a greasy bully-boy sullying a perfect carpet of fresh lain snow . . . 'Oh well, I suppose if we do go down at least we'll get to see 'em win some matches.'

I tried to strangle the fledgling notion before it fled my brain box. But it were done and could not be undone. I'd countenanced relegation. Once you stare relegation in the face can your eyes ever be averted again? West Ham's owner Eggert Magnusson also drooled the loathsome murmur: 'If we do go down we have sufficient resources to bounce back up.' I don't want to bounce back up; I don't want to bounce down. This is not a time for bouncing. When has bouncing ever been the solution? Be it with cheques or bombs it always leads to heartache. A curse on all bouncing. Except boobs, I suppose, but they're the only exception.

It were a queer night all round – 'We are West Ham's Claret 'n' Blue army' came the cry from the Centenary for periods of up to 10 minutes. Not Alan Curbishley's army, and not just because it doesn't scan well. At one point Alan Pardew's name was evoked. This for me was a stomach-churning chant, not because I don't cherish his memory but because it's too late, he's gone and can't be brought back by voodoo yelps.

The incantations became ever more intense until all were drunk in grim gallows revelry. Evangelical heads tossed back, the clap relentless as if willing West Ham to score and yet somehow delighting in failure like the embrace of death, a reaper's kiss. 'We're losing, we're going down and we don't fucking care.'

This impotent defiance, no longer about the game, but about defeat and death, heaven and hell. 'You can beat us on the pitch but you can never break our spirits.' My mate Jack turned to me and said 'I don't like losing' but while there was little heroism from the team there was heroism from the terrace in this curiously English attitude of celebrating catastrophe, this petit Dunkirk almost more invigorating than victory.

So now Matthew Upson steps into the breach: can he offer salvation or will he get devoured by a pack of stray dogs on the trip to Villa, uncomfortably close to his former home? Lucas Neill lasted about 10 seconds before hurling himself on his sword – I suppose I should be grateful that during the celebratory, player-purchase press shot while holding aloft his claret and blue shirt, flanked by Magnusson and Curbishley (still too early for Curbs), Upson's arm didn't fall off.

The transfer has reportedly left Steve Bruce suicidal, which must be a peculiar sight. One wonders what method he might employ, perhaps he'll try and batter a hole in an artery with furious fists or hurl himself off a pile of David Sullivan's porno mags.

Javier Mascherano has cleared off to Liverpool, doubtless to immediately become incontrovertibly brilliant, but Kepa Blanco has come and he has scored, and by jingo I'm in the mood for a bout of cock-eyed optimism so I'm prepared to nominate him saviour. But is that what people want? Perhaps such as we, nurtured on a diet of glorious defeat, ought to reject redemption and deliverance and let the icy caress of death lull us into a Championship slumber, because, for West Ham, all dreams must fade and die.

Troubled by Belushi's ghost and England

10 February 2007

All I know is England lost 1-0. I'm holed up in the Chateau Marmont on Sunset Boulevard and writing about a football match thousands of miles away seems berserk. I have no details of what took place at Old Trafford, all I know is the score, 1-0. I think it's safe to assume that England were listless and probably lacked ideas and creativity. I don't know if Joey Barton played or if he and Frank Lampard achieved an awkward peace and I'm rather enjoying my ignorance and the scope for speculation that affords me.

All I can be certain of is that Spain scored and England didn't. I rather fancy that England had two or three goals disallowed, among them a magnificent Jonathan Woodgate solo effort, so spectacular that it compensated for the years of injuries and redeemed him for that headband. I reckon Barton, Lampard and Steven Gerrard combined superbly for the second then scurried to the touchline to hastily scribble a first-person account of the goal for HarperCollins.

The third and most important goal I'd like to postulate was scored by Gary Lineker who sprinted down from the *Match of the Day* studio, donned the ol' No 10, but no shorts or pants, and nudged the ball past Iker Casillas with his low swinging testicles.

It would be no more peculiar than what's going on here. The news has given 24-hour coverage over to the tawdry death of Anna Nicole Smith – 'her life was just one thing after another'. So is everyone's life. That's what life is – one thing after another. 'Tis bleak indeed to witness the gleaming newscasters picking over her cadaver like a squiffy hen party of necrophiliac coroners. The culture of celebrity flings another soul on to the pyre to fuel the TV glow for another few pointless hours.

This hotel's walls bleed with history, the wails from John Belushi's ghost would keep me from sleeping were they not drowned out by the obnoxious plumbing, every drop of water accompanied by an ancient groan as the water lurches up from the bowels of Hades. God, I miss England.

Is it snowing? How quaint. How Dickensian. I miss my cat Morrissey, I miss actual Morrissey and I miss football. Of course people are aware of the impending arrival of the Beckhams – (apparently Victoria was checking out schools with a fleet of SUVs) and because celebrity is the haemoglobin of the city, people are interested but not in the football itself or its rituals and tribes. It's for children here.

This article was written out longhand and faxed to England. I'm scared to hand it over to the staff who consider most requests to be an impertinent interruption of their insouciant meditations. Plus, what if they read it? Then they'll hate me more. Perhaps it wasn't drugs that killed Belushi, maybe he just asked for an extra pillow and ended up being smothered by a vengeful chambermaid. Apparently Humphrey Bogart lived here for five years and had his own vegetable patch – it was probably the quickest way to get his hands on a potato.

Blessedly now I can hear in the next room Nik, my mate who I'm here with, browbeating a yoga teacher from Detroit into appreciating football, FOOTBALL, more than basketball. Her response was that she thinks David Beckham is handsome and that she enjoyed Zinedine Zidane's headbutt in the World Cup. What an extraordinary game it is. I wonder if events at Old Trafford bear testimony to this?

Hammers impervious to gerbils and mysticism

17 February 2007

In the book *Fever Pitch* Nick Hornby articulates the commonly held belief that there is some mystical corollary between the events in a football fan's life and the fortunes of the club that they follow. Most football fans will have at some time in their life bartered with an indifferent God over the outcome of a match, offering to trade opportunities or endure penance if only their team can get a result in return. I know I have. I would have merrily snuffed out the wiggly existence of every gerbil I owned to prolong either of Frank McAvennie's twin tenures at West Ham.

Last season whilst quivering with girly nerves in Cardiff as the Hammers played penalty-spot lotto with Liverpool in the Cup final I contemplated what I'd be prepared to relinquish, in that moment, if only Anton Ferdinand could score. I were quite prepared to forgo saucy encounters and flattery for a month, I bargained if the ball were true and our Cup adventure were not ignobly curtailed

I'd even relinquish a toe. Yes, a little toe from either foot. They look like they're being phased out by evolution anyway so it'd be an honour to swap one in return for a West Ham triumph in the Cup with a benevolent yet barmy God. Reina saved it. My toe remains, and the celestial white elephant stall where the spoils from these preposterous trades must end up was robbed of a bit of futile toot.

To people who don't follow football this twittish creed must seem right daft and I suppose it is, to force a relationship in your tiny mind betwixt your own life and the utterly abstract transpirings of 11 fellas in a field is loopy. Loopy, but forgivable when in a heightened emotional state you make these dizzy pleas, surrounded by others all willing for the same outcome, perhaps offering up digits of their own. Under those conditions 'tis understandable. But when last week I read in the *Observer*, scratched out by the inky talons of some irrelevant nerd that I, me, Russell were culpable for the dim fortunes of West Ham I was simultaneously both baffled and cross.

The nit in question suggested that West Ham's dwindling form and shameful results and my own recent success were oddly entwined, like I were a gluttonous conjoined twin to the club sucking up its nourishment to better present digital TV shows. Obviously, a simile this colourful was not employed to convey the vindictive point – the snickering hack just cobbled together clichés and puns and scurried off back to his nest to feast upon his own grunts and coax another voyeuristic squirt from his busy nib. As I'm a spiritual man (I say Hare Krishna as often as possible, sometimes even when I'm not being filmed) I'll offer the chap naught but love and consider returning to a life of self-destruction on the off chance that he's right and my ascendance is compromising West Ham's dwindling chance of survival.

West Ham lost to Watford perhaps not because of the tangible lack of goodwill between Alan Curbishley and senior players but because a few days later I was to host the Brits without any bother. Maybe Ferdinand's Bentley's window wasn't smashed out of impotent frustration by a misguided fan but because I myself on the very same day happened upon a shiny, new sixpence whilst shovelling snow.

The article, a review of the West Ham v Watford game, also implied that I should transfer allegiance to Wigan in order to avert this imagined phenomenon. Though my claret is tinged with blue I'll make the switch if it keeps us up. I'll worship Paul Jewell and stalk Emile Heskey whilst reading Orwell and guzzling pies, I'll do whatever it takes to avoid a Championship tour.

There are still 33 points to be had starting with three at The Valley as we take on Pards' Charlton next week and I've still got 10 toes. I'll do the voodoo if that'll help, what'll you do?

Bellamy's mood swings reveal artistic temperament

24 February 2007

Craig Bellamy's an interesting fella. If, as reported, his fracas with John Arne Riise was provoked by the latter's refusal to join him in a karaoke duet it is an indication that he has the incendiary temperament of a poet. I like a nice sing-song myself but don't generally penalise non-participants with a posh cosh attack. In fact, only last Christmas my cousin refused to join me in a festive rendition of Snoop and Dre's hit 'Nuthin but a Gee Thang', citing tiredness as his excuse. While I was tempted to stove his bonce in with a tennis racket I did not, out of respect for my grandmother's memory.

Every element of the Bellamy story is a joy: karaoke, golf club attack and the two protagonists scoring at Camp Nou. There's even a sub-plot where Jerzy Dudek allegedly threatened to headbutt a copper and the sublime denouement of Bellamy's golf swing celebration after his goal that bookies William Hill offered 100-1 against e'er happening.

I watched this documentary about Gazza in China and amid the bleak topography of his brain were oddities that signified the character of an artist. He spoke of a moment in his childhood where his young mind first countenanced the certainty of death. Apparently young Paul, whilst strolling with his mother, heard of the demise of a school friend's relative and immediately deduced that one day his friend, his mother and even he himself would die and that realisation spawned a cruel egg of anxiety that nestled in his belly from that day forth.

We almost expect an element of lunacy from great artists but it's surprising when encountered in a footballer, Bellamy raging around the Mediterranean coast like Hemingway walloping his colleagues about the thighs when they don't get into the spirit of things. One report said that Bellamy had initially retired after the karaoke clash but was so wound up that he couldn't sleep. I like to think of him all red, tense and prickly lying in his bed before springing to his feet, grabbing a nine-iron and embarking on his bonkers vendetta. When the news broke at the weekend it was difficult to envisage how he could ever be rehabilitated but of course, as is so often the case, if you are supremely talented you write your own rule book, and by close of business on Wednesday night Bellamy had scored and set up a second for the reluctant Sonny to his forceful Cher: Riise. On his son's 10th birthday, as if the drama could stand another delicious layer of sentiment.

Only football, it seems, can conjure these ludicrous tales, and what a season it's been for unlikely heroes and inconceivable villainy. Who would have dreamed after the World Cup winkerama that Cristiano Ronaldo would blossom into perhaps the most skilful and beloved of United's players? What loopy scriptwriter to the fates decided that Lucas Neill and Matthew Upson would manage a combined five seconds of football before being claimed by injury when they had been purchased for West Ham as a kind of pricey cavalry, but now resemble just another couple of apocalyptic horsemen.

And more ridiculous than any of the aforementioned is today's clash between Alan Pardew's Charlton and Alan Curbishley's West Ham, a London derby, a six-pointer, a relegation must-win match between two managers against their former clubs. I've placed a bet for the first time in my life, on West Ham to win, but who can really predict the outcome of this game when the season has been so daftly surreal? I might as well have put a tenner on Curbishley and Pards making love in the centre circle at the first blast of the whistle and endeavouring to tantrically continue for the full 90. That way everyone would go home satisfied.

It is time to face facts – we are all doomed

3 March 2007

From my Los Angeles hotel bedroom window I can see that Hollywood sign thing and the land of illusions of which it is a key signifier provides a necessary tonic from the excruciating fiasco of West Ham's season. Though I didn't go to the Valley of Death for the crucial match against Charlton, my mate Jack was at the scene and reported back that as West Ham deteriorated the away support grew more vociferous. For the first 10 minutes there was tension when Charlton scored, minutes later added to their tally and after 25 minutes got a third the cry of 'you're not fit to wear the shirt' rang out. At half-time there was an exodus – many fans unwilling to bear witness to the evisceration of their dreams.

During the interval, however, consensus was achieved and part two of the bleak saga was undertaken with defiant merriment and touching bluster. By the time Charlton scored their fourth, the Claret and Blue army were lost in ribald incantation – specifically the song, to the tune of 'I love you baby': 'Oh Christian Dailly, you are the love of my life, oh Christian Dailly, I'd let you shag my wife, oh Christian Dailly I want your curly hair too'.

Momentarily the Charlton fans cheered the triumph of their fourth but as the roar died down they discerned with horror that the Dailly ballad had continued unaffected by the goal. Jack says the home crowd looked on with one face of awe, unable to comprehend the unbending faith of the Irons.

It conjures in my mind the kind of relentless foe one encounters in action films who absolutely will not stop – don't turn your back on the apparent corpse of the Terminator. Even riddled with bullets and all but dismembered he'll steel himself for one last push – it's in his programming. What is it encoded so deep in the hearts of West Ham fans that they can shrug off defeat and blithely ignore humiliation?

Some of my best experiences at Upton Park took place when the Hammers have been woeful on the pitch but heroic on the terrace – it's easy to sing when you're winning as the chant suggests but it's characteristically British to celebrate failure in the way fans did at Charlton. For me it brings to mind great emblems of our nation – Falstaff, Dunkirk, Eddie 'The Eagle' Edwards. Perhaps that bellicose Norwegian commentator that banged on about Churchill and Thatcher when England lost away to Norway ought to have listed famous losers, although, of course, both Thatcher and Churchill ended their political careers in the way that all such careers must end, in failure. I think that's why I took offence when that berk from the *Observer* suggested I support Wigan, suggesting my success were inflicting some bizarre inverse photosynthesis on the team. It simply isn't done – the lyrics are quite clear: 'West Ham till I die, I'm West Ham till I die, I know I am I'm sure I am, I'm West Ham till I die'.

The evocation of the idea of death is not frivolous. We are going to die. I will die, Alan Curbishley will die, Alan Pardew will die, Anton Ferdinand will die but through West Ham we get a shot at eternal life. The Claret and Blue army will march on, infantry will come and go, generals will depart but the colour and the aim will remain. They are more constant than life, bigger than death. So Shankly's famous maxim ain't so glib – football is more important than life and death – it transcends both.

West Ham are going to be relegated. There, I've said it. But it doesn't matter, nothing matters. Jermain Defoe can score a hat-trick for Spurs tomorrow and I'll just sing – not only because I'll be jet-lagged and everyone else'll be singing, though partly. In the main it's because nothing matters. Defoe will die one day – all 22 players will expire.

At West Ham there is a campaign to abolish the Hammer of the Year award due to the team's poor form. Some say it should be awarded to Dean Ashton who's been out injured all season – it doesn't matter, give it to Deano or Leroy Rosenior or Alan Devonshire or Tony Cottee – or the fans themselves.

All that matters is that the shared dream lives on. Last time Spurs came to the Boleyn they lost their Champions League place and blamed it all on food poisoning acquired from a dodgy lasagne. I've an inkling that after Sunday it'll be West Ham fans who'll be feeling sick but after what we've swallowed this season who cares? Or maybe we'll thrash 'em and go out with some valour, but I doubt it, it just seems impossible. No one would believe it, not even here and I'm writing this in Tinsel Town, in the silvery shadow of that ridiculous sign.

Why Tony Cottee's call has left me in a dither

10 March 2007

West Ham 3 Tottenham 4. Ultimately it becomes about numbers. 4-3. Away goals four, home goals three. But of course in reality there's so much more than numbers. Emotions for a start.

I've not been moved so close to tears by a football match since Italia 90 when England lost to Germany on penalties and I was a 15-year-old schoolboy, a hormonal mess and a little bit overweight. Football was a motif for everything that I wasn't: masculine, proud, strong, inclusive.

After Spurs' fourth goal I ran the mental program that one occasionally must to defend oneself against the horrors of being a West Ham, or indeed an England fan. Right, that's it, I'm just not going to pay attention to football any more. I shan't get seduced by it. It is not a healthy pursuit for a man as emotionally volatile as me.

Regular readers of this column will remember that I said in plain black and white that Spurs would best West Ham. I had already accepted that we were going to lose that game and yet how it hurt when it actually happened. Cruel, cruel football seduced me once more into hoping that victory was possible. After Mark Noble's brilliant first goal, assisted by the unbelievable Carlos Tevez, a flicker of optimism arose within me.

But like the battered wife chained by love to her abusive partner but unable to walk away, Noble's first goal hooked me. When Tevez scored from a free kick I was in love all over again and West Ham were forgiven for the previous five defeats. Tevez's goal was the realisation of hours of tireless, dogged running. He deserved it more than anyone. When he scored and West Ham went 2-0 up, all 30,000 West Ham fans were as thrilled as Carlos himself as he pulled off his top to reveal his disgustingly fit little torso. Then, in one of the best post-goal celebrations of all time, he hurled himself into the Dr Martens Stand where I was stood, causing the kind of giddy euphoria that only the condemned can truly feel. In that brief moment of reprieve CT was lost in a sea of team-mates who accumulated around him like a beard of bees concealing the chin of a loon.

After the interval West Ham conceded a needless penalty and who should score but arch foe Jermain Defoe. I always worry that I'll meet someone like JD, Frank Lampard, Paul Ince or some other old boy that didn't leave under the best of circumstances and my natural adulation of sportsmen will overcome my filial loyalties to the club. I worry I'll end up grinning and hugging them, forgetting that it will forever sour me in the minds of the people who sit next to me in Upton Park.

Then Spurs equalised and I swear I thought, 'Bring on Bobby Zamora'. I heard the bloke behind me say there is no one on the bench to bring on, but I thought Bobby would score against Spurs. Bring him on against his old club. Minutes later Z did come on and before you know it the score was 3-2.

At this moment the release of tension was incredible. I haven't been to a football match for a very long time that has ascended (or descended, depending on your perspective) to such levels. But Spurs equalised and then Spurs scored again. I sat with a belly full of lead porridge in my guts and a head full of splintered dreams that almost emerged as tears.

The only thing that has dragged me from this defeated slumber is an answer-phone message from Tony Cottee. I have met a number of famous people but it was still extraordinary and absurd to hear the words 'Hello Russell, this is Tony Cottee. Can you give me a call regarding a charity football match?'

He went on to tell me that West Ham's team of 1986 – my favourite side, incidentally – would be involved. I gulped and gasped. Tony Cottee is inviting me to take part in a football match at Upton Park against Frank

McAvennie, Alan Dickens and perhaps even Alan Devonshire (although he didn't mention that name in the message). It could possibly be the greatest moment of my life. 'I don't know if you play football, Russell, but I was wondering if you'd like to join this match,' said Tony. Well, in short, Tony, I don't play football. I am the worst footballer on this planet. The sight of my gangly, ridiculous body simpering across the hallowed turf like something from a Tim Burton cartoon is a spectacle too ghastly to contemplate. I'm afraid to hit the ball, because of a) headaches and b) possible damage to hairstyle.

What am I going to say to Tony Cottee? I can't say no to an opportunity like this. What shall I do? However, given some of the games I've been treated to at that ground lately, perhaps I could do a lot worse than pulling on the claret and blue and standing up to face the heelers of the past.

The night I slept next to David Beckham

17 March 2007

David Beckham was in the next room to me at a Manchester hotel on Tuesday night. There were adjoining doors. I felt like I should do something, knowing he was in there either with Posh or alone sleeping, like in that Sam Taylor-Wood installation, all peaceful.

The twits I was with wanted to put a gushing note under his door, a scheme I vetoed on the grounds that it would compromise me if I ever met him. He'd always have that over me. If we met at a high-class banquet for Essex dignitaries my status would be undermined by the knowledge that I'd desperately thrust my grubby scribblings into his private quarters. It seemed uncouth – like trying to sneak my fingers up the leg of his shorts and stretching his golden balls taut.

Also, what would I put? 'Good evening David, hope you enjoyed your appearance at Old Trafford on the occasion of Manchester United versus European XI. Shame you couldn't play. Nice speech! PS: Do you miss Lakeside?'

or 'I can envisage you Dave, in there, yards from me mincing in your pristine pants – would you like me to pay you a saucy visit? Hang your panties on the door handle if yes.'

I don't think that there's anything you can write in a note to a stranger that you poke under a door that wouldn't unsettle them. I shouldn't be bothering myself with inconsequential exhibition matches in Manchester when West Ham's season lies strewn in daft tatters. Currently they await news of whether points will be deducted as a result of fielding ineligible players, Argentinians Carlos Tevez and Javier Mascherano. Alan Curbishley is sanguine about it, claiming we have no points to deduct, which is an interesting argument. In West Ham's current position they may as well deduct unicorn tears or Fabergé eggs. I myself have adapted a similarly Zen and detached stance and have prepared myself for another season of Championship football.

My methods of consolation include:

1 There are some good clubs that may be in the Championship next season if they don't get promoted or relegated. It'll be nice to go to Loftus Road for QPR and Elland Road for Leeds if they don't go down, and to receive visits from Birmingham and Sunderland if they don't go up.

2 It is more competitive, with league positions not confirmed often until the final game of the season.

3 I might actually get to see West Ham win a few games.

There was talk to the effect that if a verdict can't be reached on West Ham's points deduction before the season ends that the penalty will be carried over until the next time they're promoted – an irksome prospect but currently irrelevant. First they must be promoted and is Alan Curbishley the right man for that challenge? Hunter Davies wrote in these pages on Thursday of the characteristics required to be a great manager and in his view they need to be a bit barmy. He cited Roy Keane as an example of a good manager in waiting because of Sunderland's change in fortune this season and because of Roy's apparent air of psychopathic menace. I find it impossible to predict which players will be good coaches.

Who would have thought that dear Sir Trevor Brooking would be possessed of such venom when he took the reins at the Boleyn for the close of the 2003 season? Seeing him pumping his fist and bellowing on the touchline unnerved me. We've always known him to be such a gent, to witness him all charged and furious was disconcerting, like when my geography teacher, the usually gentle Mr Eckley, would topple into red-faced rage and pepper his rants with spittle. I'd just stand silent in the angry saliva shower and monitor the little bit of escaping wee-wee as best I could.

Perhaps that's what I should have inappropriately issued to the slumbering Becks, a request that he eschew his LA

Galaxy payday, and get back to his roots and claim his birthright as West Ham's chief. Who could know or dare to dream what uncharted depths of management skill lurk beneath his immaculately tanned facade? What cleft, disrupted dressing room could fail to be inspired by the spectacle of an incandescent Beckham yapping shrill damnations and commands whilst nimbly flicking boots into the craniums of dissenters? The solution to all West Ham's curses lay sleeping next to me in Manchester, whilst I did naught but glut myself like a chimp on cashew nuts and hotel porn.

Bring back Billie, that's all Wembley needs now

24 March 2007

I like new Wembley just fine. It seems super. Yes, it was a financial fiasco and took much too long to be completed, but this seems to be de rigueur for construction projects. I've bought a new house and am getting it done up at the moment, and I must confess that I had less of a sense of needless cash haemorrhaging when I was a devoted user of crack and heroin.

At least those illicit transactions were immediate and generally authentic. I ne'er had a drug dealer suddenly quadruple his price then suck air lethargically over his teeth before informing me that my drugs would be six months late. Why, no self-respecting junkie would tolerate it. It's a shame Wembley weren't finished last season for the Cup final between the Hammers and Liverpool. Not that Cardiff weren't a blast, it just would have been pleasant for West Ham to have played (and lost) in the inaugural finals in both Wemblies. I'm sure that's how you pluralise it.

Funny to think that the reason there's so many White Horse pubs around East London is because of the famous 1923 'White Horse Final', when Bolton triumphed over the Irons and 100,000 excess people turned up causing peaceful bother in the presence of the King, and one of the horses the mounted police were upon – I believe it were called Billie – was white. That tells us something of the power of image, there were loads of horses there that day. And policemen. And footballers. And the King of England, for Christ's sake but none of those things were deemed fit to entitle the first final because of the tyranny of iconography – that white horse looked good, plus 'the man on the white horse' is a phrase synonymous with heroism. Pegasus was one, Gandalf had one and Beckham was photographed on one a couple of weeks ago to advertise pop.

I bet that white horse Billie was a right smug bastard. I bet he shat on the supporters willy-nilly, just for a jolly, and resented turning up at a football match, thinking he were better suited to rescuing princesses and being a stud. That shouldn't be allowed either, male horses having it off for a job. It's a disgrace. My mate Matt says he rode a horse once and it was a big, muscly coward skittering about on its ridiculous tapered legs and spindle feet, too thin for its body. I'm also against them having shoes. And I'm against horseshoes being considered lucky. If they are, where's Shergar? He had four of 'em.

Photographs from that day in 1923 seem to be from another world as much as another time. All those hats and rattles and moustaches – I can't imagine those people crying or farting. One day folk will look at photographs of us, probably on digital monitors on their fingernails, and think we looked a proper sight with our tight trousers and silly hair. Actually that's just me, and I already look a bit ridiculous without the necessity for time travel.

Perhaps in the future England will have a team that can qualify for major championships without turning us into a nation of quivering, accusatory paranoids. Can we get a result in Israel today?

Confidence in the national side is low after Eriksson's reign and McClaren's appointment and subsequent losses. From where do we draw optimism for today's tie? As per bloody usual players that are great for their clubs look chastened and curtailed by the emblazoning of the three lions 'pon their boobs – Lampard, Gerrard, Ferdinand etc – so it is to the novel that we turn for hope, young Aaron Lennon, AJ and Preston NE's Nugent.

After the season I've endured at club level I'm kind of immune to disappointment. Unless Rooney takes to the pitch in lingerie singing 'Oklahoma!' I don't think my expectations can be further wounded. If they don't win or at least draw today the hullabaloo will be renewed and we shall holler for McClaren's bonce, but with whom do we replace him? Though the years have onward rolled and much has changed since 1923 one thing remains the same: the significance of image. I, for one, am prepared to revise my antipathy towards things equine and demand

Billie the white horse be made manager of England. He'll look great in photos, he'll be handy if there's crowd trouble, and if it don't work we can put him out to stud – and I don't think we'd get away with that with McClaren.

I sympathise with McClaren – but he is crap

31 March 2007

'Gentlemen, if you want to write whatever you want to write, you can write it because that is all I am going to say. Thank you. Nothing concerns me about what people write or say. What matters is what is on the inside.'

Right. Let's break that down. 'Gentlemen' – well, that's nice for a start cos it's polite. At least McClaren didn't commence his lachrymose diatribe with 'wankers' or 'you bully-boys'. The fact that he addressed the conference as 'gentlemen' makes me feel a bit sad. There's a kind of spurned and tearful dignity to good manners under pressure. Plus he always looks a bit red anyway, which always gives the impression of a man on the brink of a tantrum.

'If you want to write whatever you want to write, you can write it.' This is the most grammatically challenging passage. The sentence appears to be eating itself and regenerating as it tumbles from his chops. 'If you want to write whatever you want to write.' That statement is beyond tautology and made me confused and happy as I watched it bluster forth. He looked like a panicking supply teacher fumbling for authoritative rhetoric inside his parched and nervous gob. And perhaps that's what he is. He certainly appears to be out of his depth with matters both on and off the field. When Fergie loses patience with journalists it's intimidating, when Keegan did, it was touching, McClaren's outburst was just embarrassing. I do want to write whatever I'm going to write so I'm going to write it. Steve McClaren seems like a nice bloke, so I feel a bit mean. Also I've had moments where I've felt a bit victimised by tabloids. Nothing remotely on this scale – they've never delighted in dreaming up nicknames for me – they just say I'm a randy oddball, and it never stops hurting.

I don't think any of us were satisfied by his appointment because his record at Boro wasn't fantastic, Ferguson implied he was inadequate, there were more exciting candidates and he lacks charisma. Quentin Crisp said that charisma is the ability to influence without logic. I don't think McClaren can influence with or without logic. He doesn't seem to inspire his team, the Press have made him a laughing-stock and the fans don't like him. These problems combined are unassailable. I'm not a football expert, however I can see that it might have been good to give Gareth Barry a run-out so someone on the left was in position against Israel, not to play so many long balls with forwards like Rooney and AJ who need the ball in 'the channel' and to stop selecting and playing with tangible trepidation. Where's the flair for God's sake?

'Nothing concerns me about what people write or say.' Well, that simply isn't true, it obviously hurts him. If he didn't care, he wouldn't have mentioned it – like me with ice hockey and tampon prices. I never think about them so it never comes up except for just then as an example of things that don't concern me. McClaren said the word 'write' four times in his TV breakdown and he's had his teeth Tipp-Exed, not the act of a man impervious to public perception.

'What matters is what's on the inside.' I'm with him there – that is what matters. Life is transient and the material world is but an illusion, only love is real. But that's when you take the infinite and the eternal as your sole and absolute context. Those rules do not apply to football. In football it's what's on the pitch that matters and who's in the team and what they write in the papers and what your nickname is. And none of those things look good. In cosmic terms Steve McClaren is a perfect child of God but in international football terms he needs to look inside himself and see if he has what matters.

I dangled sex-aids through riot van windows

7 April 2007

America likes to think that where it leads, all other nations follow. This seemingly self-important world-view exists presumably because that's pretty much what happens. But though we are all perfectly happy to embrace the nation's great advances eagerly – *Friends*, Starbucks, Coke Zero, the South Beach Diet – we seem less inclined to learn from their mistakes.

Perhaps we ought not be surprised by reports of violent skirmishes, conflict and aggressive policing at European matches – it's not so long ago that our continent was torn apart by war. It seems that conflagration is often sub-cutaneous at football and that the essential thrill of attending live matches is its fusion with repressed tension.

I've never been caught up in trouble at football. In the days before all-seat stadiums, when I'd stand behind the goal, it was different to now – more smokey, blokey, belchey, cackley, whites-of-the-eyes-starey-scary and being jostled and knocked was a constant part of the experience. But I never found myself, all podgy and 11, bellowing 'You want some?!' into the face of a Millwall fan or the visor of a riot cop. Although I recall the back of my jacket once being singed by a fan's lighter as I chubbily observed West Ham v Forest, it scarcely counts as hooliganism. Bill Hicks joked that even the word 'hooligan' sounded comic and ineffectual, like they were all malnourished and pale, and remarked that even the toughest 'firm' would struggle against the Crips or the Bloods.

I used to attend protests and marches and often they'd tumble into riots and I must confess that as a younger, stupider man, I found them quite exhilarating. May Day 2001 in London was berserk. I was a junkie then and working for MTV and I dragged a film crew with me to document events. I was astonished and enchanted by this skinhead lad in an England shirt that I met who clearly wasn't there because of passionately held, articulate beliefs on the nefarious nature of corporate culture but just because he'd recognised a legitimate opportunity to smash shop windows and have a go at the Old Bill.

I reflected at the time that he had as much right to be there as the hardline anarchists of the notorious Black Block because his grievances were not theoretical but practical. He was not a university educated romantic revolutionary. He was just angry and had found an outlet for his rage. I got into all sorts of silly bother that day dangling sex-aids through riot van windows, trying to organise a protesters v coppers football match in Piccadilly (inspired by the World War One Christmas Eve truce) and stripping naked at the statue of Eros.

I was surrounded by police and baited them with my curiously (given the location) unerotic striptease. They watched with a kind of bored indifference till I pulled down my Che Guevara Y-fronts, then folded in around me like dough. I've watched footage from that day and it's intriguing to witness the police transform from passive sentries at a madman's sex dance into truculent storm-troopers dragging me off, all nude and twitching.

I feigned an epileptic fit to buy myself some time, an embarrassing and galling spectacle only really trumped by the sight of my silly, chilly, tiny drugged willy, unaware of how it would humiliate me in years to come by cropping up in archive photos. It's bigger now. Honest. I'm considering posing nude just to vindicate myself to the Met. Perhaps I could team up with them and do a calendar.

I ended up being charged with criminal damage and indecent exposure. The charges were eventually dropped, blessedly, because I would've hated to watch the CCTV footage back in court. I've never been arrested abroad. I imagine it's awfully traumatic, and it seems that due to the enduring reputation of English fans, police in Europe can be frightfully over zealous. The trouble in Rome and Seville is upsetting but initial reports suggest that our fans were bawdy but bearable and that the intimidating accoutrements and attitude of authorities at the stadiums exacerbated the situation.

But at least these days it's largely peaceful football matches being interrupted by violence as opposed to great big bloody wars being interrupted by a festive game of football.

Brutal laptop reality destroys my island fantasy

21 April 2007

Oh I get it, wait until I'm safely tucked up in my 'Prison Paradise' Hawaii, and then have English football transform into the most thrilling, rewarding game on earth. Man United v Roma? 7-1? Oh come on, it's absurd. I'm on an island where I can't even get my thirsty, deprived little fists on English newspapers and enjoy the analysis, let alone actually watch matches. Oh what I wouldn't give to have grimy, inky fingers from holding the prestigious pages you now grip – or the dear old *Sun*. I'd be happy with the *Telegraph* and *Star* for God's sake.

Instead of which, I am trapped amidst this tedious beauty reading about West Ham beating Arsenal at the Emirates on a laptop screen – the horror, the indignity, it's so un-English. Of course whilst abroad, I become so aware of my national identity as almost to become a poisonous racist or at least social shipwreck. I'm considering wearing a knotted hanky on my head and eating bangers and mash on the beach whilst rolling my eyes at the turtles and surfers.

If surfing had not been invented and I found myself in the ocean with a surfboard, which would exist without function in the parallel universe of my devising, I would after perhaps an hour's endeavour deem surfing to be utterly impossible and implausible. The bonkers fact that everyone here can do it seems to me a denial of the laws of physics – I might just as well design a sport that involves the practitioners wearing pig's-trotter goggles and playing billiards with their shins.

Perhaps this loopy event might cause me less arse-ache than following the team I'm chained to by heredity and geography. West Ham's brief, triumphant run collapsed after they'd done enough to inspire some dumb optimism in me, making a mockery of the practice that I'm sure a lot of belligerent football supporters undertake – particularly if they suddenly have time on their hands, stranded yards from the location where *Lost* is filmed – I've been studying the fixtures of my own team, Wigan, Charlton and Sheff United and calculating a points prognosis based on my results predictions.

Unfortunately this system is impeded by the idiotic bias of the practitioner. Using this device I swiftly deduced that Sheffield United and Wigan would be joining Watford for a Championship jaunt next season because I am incapable of excluding aspiration from the process. According to my system the Hammers will triumph at Bramall Lane and then hold Chelsea to a draw at Upton Park, securing four points from a possible six. Fine, except the relentless march of time and truth has brutally presented me with an unpalatable brace of thrashings from those encounters.

When poring over the fixtures I convince myself that I'm being objective and even now, after the fallibility of the system has been made painfully evident, I still find myself looking at forthcoming games and thinking 'Ooh, I think Everton at home should be three points' and 'Oh, I see Charlton and Sheffield United are playing each other – they'll hopefully field teams ridden with convicted sex offenders and face an automatic 20-point deduction leaving West Ham in the clear, wahoo!'

I suppose the inevitable relegation of West Ham will seem more bearable from the other side of Earth, just sad text messages from friends and Internet-derived news. Not for me the doleful trudge down Green Street and agonising colour photos adorning glib red tops. I'll be witnessing the fall from a hammock drenched in delicious clichés.

I heard today that coconuts kill more people than crocodiles (than are killed by crocodiles, not 20 people a year and 17 crocodiles in the coconut league of death. I don't know the stats for crocodile deaths – I don't have that much free time). I shall have to keep my wits about me, I don't need the word 'coconut' cropping up in my obituary . . . 'Ballbag comedian killed by falling coconut whilst lamenting West Ham's relegation'. Tragically I wouldn't be able to read my own obituary because you can't get the papers here. And I'd be dead.

It's not natural, but by jingoism I love Chelsea

28 April 2007

I don't know if I ought to admit this, it seems to be a taboo on a par with snogging pets which I would never admit to – no, that love will never dare speak its name – probably because 'that love's' got a gob full of Winalot to ensnare a randy Scottie dog. Just to clarify, I don't snog my pet or anyone else's and that's why I'd never admit to it. I just wanted to raise the notion of the forbidden, and in so doing have probably placed my relationship with my cat, Morrissey, in jeopardy.

I dare say some people on reading what I'm about to render would prefer I, nightly, dressed Morrissey in little cat suspenders and stilettos and emptied myself of the burden of my masculinity into his perfect fizzog – such is the profundity of my forthcoming admission. So, here it is: When English teams play in Europe, even Chelsea, I don't want them to lose. Actually, I want them to win, in spite of the fact that as a West Ham fan (I know I mention this every week but one must cater for the uninitiated, though we can perhaps safely assume that an unsuspecting reader, happening upon this column for the first time would unlikely have got past the earlier, revolting depiction of feline fellatio) at every home game, in all but one of which Chelsea are absent, I am obliged to invite them through song to 'stick their blue flag up their arse'.

Now, Chelsea play Liverpool in their semi-final (I know that's obvious but again, assume ignorance) and you might imagine that my personal allegiances would lead me to favour a victory for the Reds, and typically they would but I rather like the idea of an epic Manchester United v Chelsea triptych as the finale to the season. Plus, whilst I'm making ill-judged confessions, I like Jose Mourinho. I like his arrogance, his intellect, his determination and, yes, I think he's handsome. This is not to the detriment of my love of West Ham – two crossed Irons is the only tattoo I'd consider having – but when it comes to European competition I like to see English sides do well, Scottish an' all – I was sorry to see Celtic go out to Milan, who I hope lose to United on Wednesday giving us an all-English final.

My patriotism has been enhanced by my current period of prolonged absence. I'm in Hawaii making a film and shall be here for two months. I think army recruitment officials oughtn't focus on depressed British towns but instead our preferred holiday destinations because I'm usually quite an anti-establishment type of fella but out here I weep at any mention of the Albion and would happily kill a man for a slur on Princess Anne, let alone

Her Majesty. God forbid anyone should utter a negative word about dear Di – I'd carve the lyrics of 'Rule Britannia' into their chops with a sharpened pineapple.

I suppose the logic of my position (on football, not the aforementioned hypothetical Royalist revenge beatings) is that if English football is proven to be the best in Europe West Ham's current position is somehow more tenable – 'Why, if they were in Serie A they'd be cleaning up.' The charges they're facing wouldn't look out of place in the corrupt Italian league of last season. Poor ol' West Ham, who'd've thought the first pair of corporately owned, brokered-in-a-deal-by-a-prospective-new-chairman-superstar, South Americans they purchased would have led to such trouble? By the time you read this a decision will have been reached on the Hammers' punishment. I hope it was financial rather than a points deduction, let's get relegated on our own 'merit'.

I personally think the way the season has panned out is punishment enough – Pardew's gone, we're going down and Mascherano has cleared off to Anfield to immediately and predictably become brilliant. What a fiasco. So surely I'm entitled to a modicum of guilty, patriotic pride when English teams triumph abroad? Please, your Honour? Why, there's not a Uefa-appointed, three-man panel on earth that would convict me.

Daaaaaaaave Whelan, is a whiner, is a whiner

5 May 2007

Dave Whelan, the chairman of Wigan Athletic, in my view, can eff right off. I'm proper brassed off (at first I was just cheesed off, then browned off till eventually I reached the summit – brassed off) with all of West Ham's fellow relegation strugglers clamouring for a points deduction after last week's tribunal decreed that a £5.5m fine would be penalty enough. Six clubs in total, naturally the ones vying with the Irons for a place in the Championship, all met up, like castrato assassins, thumbing their impotent nubs, plotting litigation against a club that have endured a season of unremitting punishment. Eff off.

Where would it all end? If they successfully brought about legal action to convert West Ham's fine to a points deduction West Ham could protest about that and bring action until the fact that this carousel of legal activity was once 'the beautiful game' would be forgotten in the blur. It's interesting though to learn how your team is regarded by folk outside the clan. I was tickled to hear Whelan refer to West Ham as 'a big club' and a beneficiary of favouritism. Perhaps one judges the size of the team one follows in the context of the chief rivals encountered. In the Premiership in London, that's Chelsea, Arsenal and Spurs – all teams that in terms of silverware and funds overshadow West Ham. Not in the area of support though, no, nor in calibre of supporter – that's where the Hammers tower, precisely because we have to endure defeat, ignominy and poverty (not me personally any more, I've recently acquired a nest-egg).

AFC Wimbledon have suffered a deduction this season for comparable offences and this, along with the demented belief that Wigan or Watford, had they similarly transgressed would have their season's points tally reduced by half and be forced to play their remaining games with teams comprising drugged woodland animals, is the foundation for Whelan's spiteful scheming. He can eff right off. He's simply a bit peeved that West Ham now have a decent chance of avoiding relegation by, horror of horrors, winning football matches. Call me a cad but this is the fashion in which I like to see the Premiership conducted. Perhaps Whelan (and I'm fighting powerful urges to grant him an alliterative nickname now, eg, Whining Whelan) would prefer it if instead of facing Bolton at Upton Park on Saturday, West Ham appeared at the Old Bailey and had Rumpole or Judge Pickles decide the outcome of the match using their genitals as a sexy divining rod of soccer justice? I reckon he would, I reckon he'd get off on it.

I myself am a bit peeved that Manchester United didn't

win in Milan giving us an all-English final but I shan't dwell on it or start a barmy campaign to have Kaka and Ancelotti appear before Chelmsford magistrates' court and be given community service. I shall just wish Liverpool all the best and hope they bring home the cup, even though they prevented West Ham winning their only trophy for 25 years by beating them on penalties in Cardiff last year.

I was disappointed after that match and on the way home, with Olympian and chum Ade Adepitan, the two of us grieved and consoled ourselves with the knowledge that football can be painful and seemingly unfair, but we didn't try to raise the ghost of Biblical adjudicator King Solomon and ask him if he could stop Stevie Gerrard scoring just as stoppage time began. It's just not on.

West Ham's purchase of Tevez and Mascherano was obviously, to some degree, irregular, but they have been fined five-and-a-half million quid as a result and it's not as if the transaction was an unqualified success – the whole thing's been a right balls up, as was the sacking of Pardew and the bonds scheme which sold the club to the fans a few years back, and the enormous expenditure on a daft model of a boat that adorns the club's foyer. West Ham's only crime is that they are a shambolic club. And that is also their punishment.

Cooing over Carlos has made me feel 15 again

12 May 2007

I don't want Carlos Tevez to leave West Ham. I really don't. Like how I didn't want Paolo Di Canio to leave, I feel a pang, an impotent pang, a hopeless sense of foreboding, the futility of trying to reject the inevitable. I don't want to lapse into a fruity ode or juvenile love letter but I can't ignore these feelings. . .

He plays with such fervid determination and skill, how can he be replaced? And how can a player who, when he chases a ball, inadvertently seems to evoke the image of his deprived youth, be running towards a future beyond the Boleyn Ground?

It's beautiful when a footballer achieves effortless rapport with a crowd and Tevez has done this. He has become the embodiment of West Ham's struggle for survival, itself an emblem for the countless battles, trivial and awesome, we conduct throughout our days, catharsis and rehearsal for the struggle we all must face when eventually we die.

Oh Christ, I've gawn all maudlin, I am 15 once more and gushing unwelcome love and unsolicited sperm, I'll not condemn myself. Even Freddy Shepherd, when forced to countenance the departure of a cherished star, in his case Michael Owen, resorts to the hormonal yawps of a teenage jerk – 'He should pledge himself to us, no one else wants him.' That's pretty emotional – he should be shrieking that sentence outside a kebab shop on a bleary Saturday night with sick on his chin and his mini-skirt pinched between his bum cheeks: 'I love you Michael, don't leave me – I can change. . .'

With Tevez there is no evidence of impending departure in his demeanour or his game. He plays like it will last forever, like there could be no other club. How do they do that? Is it really just about money and ambition? I suppose it is. What right have I to be disappointed?

I allow my life to be governed by those factors, tucking the revolution down my pants to make my package more impressive whilst all the while pursuing women and power. But I expect more from footballers. Tevez was scarred as a boy and at Boca Juniors, his first club, was offered cosmetic surgery to correct it. Carlos refused out of integrity and self-acceptance – that's lovely isn't it? If I get a pimple I refuse to leave the house. It's odd how I relate to footballers – he's only 23, if I met him in another context I'd flip him a shiny penny, ruffle his hair and give him some tips on dames but as it is I'm forever frozen in adoring childhood peering, from my father's side, at these men, as fierce and loud as when horses rumble by.

I only have the luxury of this current fixation as it now seems (don't jinx it, don't jinx it) that West Ham may survive after an implausible run inspired by Carlos and now only (ONLY!) require a draw against Man United at Old Trafford to be guaranteed of safety. I'm a bit miffed that Ferguson plans to field a full strength team – what a bloody cheek, those lads ought be resting after a gruelling season of triumph, they've the inaugural Wembley Cup final to consider.

Alex Ferguson appears more approachable and avuncular lately, I wonder why that is? It coincides with the Rev Ian Paisley becoming a bit more jolly an' all. Perhaps there is hope for the world if these two formidable men, who forever seemed on the precipice of hurling chalk at some bothersome pupil, now have the bearing of a pair of Debenham's Father Christmases. So that's a reason for optimism. And after the irreplaceable Paolo we were blessed with Carlos, the lineage may continue, and they needn't all be Latino, these saviours, these heroes. Mark Noble radiates promise and his surname couldn't be more encouraging.

I'm getting bored of baloney and tired of turtles

19 May 2007

Frequently in my life there have been occasions where I've had cause to suspect that the very laws of physics have bent themselves to inconvenience me, events so preposterous that I fancy God to be some malevolent trickster perched on a cloud piddlin' ill fortune and rubbing his holy hands with glee at his divine meddling.

Like when my foot was run over by a taxi that I was sat in, I thought, 'Well, this can't happen every day.' Or when I awoke naked atop a double bed in a squat in Kentish Town, occupied by a dozen baffled refugees, when I distinctly recalled dozing off in the arms of a Norwegian woman called Petra. Or consider the evening where I was propositioned in the lavvy of the pub in which I worked by a horny-handed builder with the line, delivered in a heavy Cork accent: 'I sensed chemistry between us when you passed me my crisps, how 'bout a kiss?'

The last two happened on the same day. All the aforementioned made me query the logic of the universe and sent me inwardly spiralling, questioning all that I'd previously known to be true – 'I bet that don't happen to everyone else,' I'd think. My feelings of cosmic persecution are similarly roused by the lingering threat that West Ham's extraordinary season, a tale of triumph snatched from the foaming gnashers of inevitable, incontrovertible defeat, could still yet magically dwindle into failure by means never before encountered.

What? We win seven of our last nine, including a final-day victory at Old Trafford, and we might still get relegated by a brand new, retrospective point deduction after a £5.5m fine, when the season has concluded? I don't think the breaches are that bad and people that keep harpin' on about 'em are right squares. U18? B12? They sound like Nationalist factions that are best ignored. The main thrust of the argument as far as I can see, from behind my blinkers, is that you aren't allowed to have a third party in a position where they can influence club activity as MSI, purportedly, were as they were renting us the players.

West Ham pleaded guilty and were appropriately penalised and that should be the end of it. I don't think it's that bad, how does the breach favour the Hammers anyway? What, is Kia Joorabchian of MSI gonna phone up Curbishley and go: 'Here, you might wanna tell Tevez to play football really well, you know, with a sincere, almost spiritual, devotion and scoring an' that.' 'Brilliant,' Curbs would respond. 'Until now we'd been playing him out of position with red hot gravel in his boots.'

Actually, the second bit's not impossible at West Ham. Greavesy mentions similar practices as a regular part of training during his time at Upton Park. It's probably a good rule that outside entities cannot exert force over clubs. In these days of oligarchs, consortia and agents it's likely to occur but ought to be kept to a minimum, and the largest fine in history is probably sufficient incentive to comply.

If Jose Mourinho is found to have brought his dog into the country without observing the correct procedure, perhaps John Terry should be made to play all Chelsea's away games wearing women's knickers and whenever Frank Lampard takes a corner he should have to breast-feed the opposition's fans.

I imagine the issue will be discussed rationally on the consistently excellent *Soccer AM* this morning, in my humble view the best football programming available, which I deeply miss while in Hawaii. That looks stupid written down but it's true – you can only marvel at turtles for so long. It never patronises its viewers and it's honest, bright and in tune with the people it caters for.

I was on it once and embarrassed myself a bit by falling over during a headstand, which was another occasion on which I insisted the universe was conspiring against me. This will doubtless be eclipsed on today's show as

I understand Noel Gallagher, who has recently come out to me as bisexual, is guesting and will probably spend the entire show evading questions on the FA Cup final, preferring instead to lunge across the delightful Helen Chamberlain and fondle the thighs of dear Tim Lovejoy, which will make for fine viewing and be further evidence that worldly affairs are being maliciously directed by loonies on Olympus.

All that's going on and I'm stuck here like Robinson Crusoe wondering if next season the Almighty, through his emissary on earth, Sepp Blatter, will ordain that some of West Ham's hard-won points must be hoovered up into the heavens condemning them to purgatory.

Is Beckham really the equal of Sir Cliff Richard?

9 June 2007

I've not done my column for a couple of weeks on account of me workload here in Hawaii, making this film. I still read the *Guardian*, though, even when I'm not in it (what dedication) and got off on reading 'Russell Brand is away' at the bottom of the page, like 'Jeffrey Bernard is unwell'. It conjured in me a reverie in which I were a wandering correspondent slumped in a Kasbah having traded my typewriter for gin.

It's been interesting to view the latest instalment of the Beckham saga from American soil, his reinstatement first to the team then to his position of national darling and soccer-Christ. I didn't see the game against Estonia but he was predictably instrumental setting up the second two goals and I bet he looked dashing into the bargain.

But, remotely viewed, the ensuing hyperbole becomes evermore preposterous – I've read in English papers, honestly, HONESTLY, that he should be knighted and ought now be emblazoned on banknotes. Where do we go from here? What if we qualify for the Championships, will we make him head of state? And if we reach the final ought we demand scientists flood the globe with his oiled and shaven clones craving as a nation just a moment at his teat, an army of unctuous, bald, genetically engineered gods lactating ambrosia into our awed Pac-man gobs?

Now I yield to no man in my adulation for David Beckham: he's handsome, vain, talented and from Essex, all the things a man ought to be, but can he replace Dickens on a tenner? Or be Sir Cliff Richard's equal in the title league? Perhaps he can. Our opinions oscillate as regularly as the mechanism within Big Ben (which I'm campaigning to have renamed 'Big Beckham Clock'), a fact from which Frank Lampard is said to draw solace having been relentlessly harangued throughout the friendly against Brazil.

'Tis said that it's an accepted part of international football, the ol' vilification and victimisation of a selected player and as a West Ham fan (have I mentioned that?) 'Lamps' ought to be the very kind of player I'd delight in loathing: he's an ex-Hammer, he's moved to a bigger club and gone on to be a successful member of the England set up, he's detested at Upton Park and was sporadically despised even before he left, initially because of Frank senior's presumed influence and then because of perceived inconsistency and for some barmy reason being fat. It must be really horrible, I'm sure he's trying his hardest.

It's a daft element of the game and I just did a quick scan of the ol' noggin to see if I'd ever been involved. The scan results were positive. I joined in this season with a chorus of 'Jermain Defoe is a c**t' against Spurs, but he's on an opposing side and, again, is ex-West Ham. I yelped approvingly when, last time West Ham were relegated, a bloke behind us viscerally screamed 'Roeder you c**t, you've killed West Ham', but Roeder had appallingly mismanaged the club. And I have been complicit in the awkward silences that have greeted Nigel Reo-Coker's name over the course of the season, but he was adored and wanted to leave.

In all three examples I can think of justification and Lampard has said in his case it's probably because he's stopped scoring. I think it might also be because people think he oughtn't be automatic choice to partner Gerrard in the middle and that there is a perception that Steve McClaren has 'undroppable' players of which he is one.

I've been reading *Boys of '86* by Tony McDonald and Danny Francis, which documents the season in which West Ham achieved their highest league position and I almost drowned in nostalgia. The book is lovingly compiled and a joy to read, especially if you witnessed Frank McAvennie, Tony Cottee and Alan Devonshire play. What is astonishing is how the game has changed in such a short period of time. Top-flight football was seemingly founded on egg and chips, beer and travelling to matches on the Tube.

The players interviewed within speak of camaraderie and loyalty, which is anathema in the game just a few years later. I was touched by the testimony of Alan Dickens who I remember as a very skilful good passer of the ball (my mate Jack said he liked how he played with his head up like a giraffe, I said Thomas Hearns) who now drives a cab and kind of drifted out of the game after an unfulfilling move to Chelsea.

After the tremendous season that the book covers, West Ham's fortune, along with Dickens' form, dwindled and I can remember being at Upton Park, aged about 12 and feeling antipathy towards Dickens. I don't recall if there were any hollering but had there been, I would certainly have meekly joined in. I felt a bit guilty when I read that he was actually a very sensitive man and that it had really hurt him when the crowd turned. Of course today's players are all billionaires who can purchase glee by the barrel if they so choose but they are still human, with sparks of divinity glowing beneath the layers of Prada and Bentley and I for one will be offering compassion to the c★★ts.